CONSUMER BEHAVIOUR

MS-61

Notes For

Master of Busines Administration [MBA]

Useful For

IGNOU, KSOU (Karnataka), Bihar University (Muzaffarpur), Nalanda University, Jamia Millia Islamia, Vardhman Mahaveer Open University (Kota), Uttarakhand Open University, Kurukshetra University, Seva Sadan's College of Education (Maharashtra), Lalit Narayan Mithila University, Andhra University, Pt. Sunderlal Sharma (Open) University (Bilaspur), Annamalai University, Bangalore University, Bharathiar University, Bharathidasan University, HP University, Centre for distance and open learning, Kakatiya University (Andhra Pradesh), KOU (Rajasthan), MPBOU (MP), MDU (Haryana), Punjab University, Tamilnadu Open University, Sri Padmavati Mahila Visvavidyalayam (Andhra Pradesh), Sri Venkateswara University (Andhra Pradesh), UCSDE (Kerala), University of Jammu, YCMOU, Rajasthan University, UPRTOU, Kalyani University, Banaras Hindu University (BHU) and all other Indian Universities.

GullyBaba Publishing House Pvt. Ltd.

ISO 9001 & ISO 14001 CERTIFIED CO.

Regd. Office:
2525/193, 1st Floor, Onkar Nagar-A,
Tri Nagar, Delhi-110035
(From Kanhaiya Nagar Metro Station Towards Old Bus Stand)
Call: 9991112299, 9312235086
WhatsApp: 9350849407

Branch Office:
1A/2A, 20, Hari Sadan,
Ansari Road, Daryaganj,
New Delhi-110002
Ph.011-45794768
Call & WhatsApp:
8130521616,8130511234

E-mail: hello@gullybaba.com, **Website**: GullyBaba.com

New Edition

Author: Gullybaba.com Panel

Disclaimer

Although the author and publisher have made every effort to ensure that the information in this notes is correct, the author and publisher do not assume and hereby disclaim any liability to any party for any loss, damage, or disruption caused by errors or omissions, whether such errors or omissions result from negligence, accident, or any other cause.

If you find any kind of error, please let us know and get reward and or the new notes free of cost.

The notes is based on IGNOU syllabus. This is only a sample. The notes/author/publisher does not impose any guarantee or claim for full marks or to be passed in exam. You are advised only to understand the contents with the help of this notes and answer in your words.

All disputes with respect to this publication shall be subject to the jurisdiction of the Courts, Tribunals and Forums of New Delhi, India only.

About Publisher

Gullybaba Publishing House is the brainchild of Mr Dinesh Verma, his name alone evokes profound respect and admiration. He is the pioneer of providing quality materials to the students of IGNOU because, having been a student of IGNOU, he understood the difficulty and pain of the non-availability of quality materials himself. He is serving the students with the following services:

EXAM-SUCCESS GUIDES

Important questions, solved question papers, guess papers - all in one! to score good marks in lesser time and effort.

FREE BOOK

As our love and care for our students, here is a Free Gift – A Famous Book "Secrets to Pass IGNOU Exams with Less Study" for you. You can download it now! https://www.gullybaba.com/ignou-free/

YOUR CONTRIBUTION TO MOTHER-EARTH

When you read our books, you save our mother earth as we use recycled paper to make these books. On every purchase, we contribute something to plant a plant.

SOLVED ASSIGNMENTS PDFs / HAND-WRITTEN

Best and genuine solved assignments PDFs you can instantly download from Gullybaba.com or our App.

PROJECT REPORTS/SYNOPSIS

Best Quality No-Rejection projects/synopsis by professionals researchers in ready to refer format.

MOBILE APP

You can download 'Gullybaba' app from Google Play Store to enjoy all above services at one place.

Why Gullybaba's IGNOU Help Books

Is Fear of Exams making you stressful? Are you not getting good marks in your IGNOU exams? Are you looking for sure-shot solution get ahead in your IGNOU studies? Look no further than the answer: Gullybaba.com! With our expertly crafted course help-books, you'll be ready to face any exam with ease-guaranteed. What's more, we offer a huge discount on IGNOU Help Books Combo Deals – Save BIG.

Now, complete IGNOU courses more quickly and with Good Marks in Lesser Time & Effort.

Home Delivery of GPH Books

You can order Gullybaba Books online from Gullybaba.com or Gullybaba App. We dispatch books on the same day of receiving the order through our fastest courier partners.
You can also order books through WhatsApp on 9350849407 or by email at order@gullybaba.com.
We also provide "Cash On Delivery" through our courier partners and sometimes Govt. Postal Department.

Important Note to Sellers

Selling this book on any online platform like Amazon, Flipkart, Shopclues, Rediff, etc. without prior written permission of the publisher is prohibited and hence any sales by the SELLER will be termed as ILLEGAL SALE of GPH Books which will attract strict legal action against the offender.

Notable Information

An attempt has been carefully made to present this book more useful and meet the requirement and challenges of the course prescribed by IGNOU University. We hope that this effort will fulfil the readers' expectations and help them excel in exams. Referring to University study material alongside this book is like "icing on the cake".

We wish you a successful and rewarding career. If you have any feedback to improve our books/products, please email at feedback@gullybaba.com. Because we believe, "Feedback is breakfast of champions" and our readers are our strength.

Table of Contents

Question Papers

1

Consumer Behaviour: Issues & Concepts

Q1. Till a few years ago, the ready-made clothes markets in India was limited to a few companies offering men's shirts and trousers in a few instances. But today, Vimal, Bata, Madura Coats and many others big companies have launched entire ranges of ready to wear garments for men and women. Can you identify some key variables of individual determinants and external environment responsible for this change.

Or

Explain the characteristics of culture and the influence the culture has on consumer decision-making.

Ans. Variables of Individual Determinants

- **Motivation and Involvement:** All of us are consumers, within a given society all of us have the same 00alternatives to choose from and yet no two consumers may exhibit identical consumer behaviour. The reason for this is that each one of us is a unique individual with a unique set of needs, desires, and motivation. Motivation is that internal force which arouses or activates some need and provides direction of behaviour towards fulfilment of the need. A motivation may be physiological in nature directed towards fulfilment of biological needs such as hunger and thirst other motivations are psychological in nature focussing on the satisfaction of psychological desires such as the desire for seeking status, job satisfaction, or achievement. Everyone has both physiological and psychological motivations, but we each fulfil them in different ways. One consumer satisfies his thirst by drinking water, the second quenches it by having a Thums Up, the third drinks Bisleri Mineral Water while a fourth prefers soda. For one consumer, buying a Delux Maruti car is a way of seeking status, another satisfies his want for status by becoming a member of the best club in town, while for a third having a credit card is a status symbol. Different methods of satisfaction of motivations is adopted because of the differing level of personal involvement in various activities. Involvement refers to the personal relevance or importance of a product or service that a consumer perceives in a given situation. For a professional photographer the choice of a camera is a consumer behaviour situation of involvement because the camera is his most important professional tool. The photographer would be motivated to buy the best possible camera, irrespective of the price tag. For another consumer, a camera is just a means of recording important family events and just about any camera which is convenient to handle would fill the need. High involvement leads to a highly motivated state of mind as in case of the professional photographer. High involvement and high motivation lead to a consumer behaviour process which is distinctly different from that of a low involvement and low motivation.

- **Attitudes:** Attitudes are our learned predispositions towards objects, people and events. Attitudes guide our orientation towards these. It is our attitudes which influence how we respond to different products and services. Attitudes are not inborn or innate in us. Rather they are learnt from people around us. Till a few years ago most housewives had a negative attitude towards frozen, dehydrated or instant food. But today, with more women joining the work force, such products are viewed as a convenience and instant, quick to cook meals are looked upon favouurably. Similarly, our attitude towards saving is undergoing radical changes. Instead of saving and leading a simple, frugal life, people prefer to have a better lifestyle today rather than save for tomorrow. Our attitudes influence our purchase decisions and consumer behaviour. An attitude which is averse to risk taking will never make for a consumer investing his money in shares and stocks, such a consumer would always prefer 'safe' investments even if though rate of return may be comparatively lower.
- **Personality and Self-concept:** Personality is the sum total of the unique individual characteristics that make each one of us what we are. It provides a framework within which a consistent behaviour can be developed. Self-concept or self-image is the way we perceive ourselves in a social framework. We always tend to buy only those products and services which we think fit or match with our personality. Marketers also try to give a distinct image or personality to their products which is as close as possible to that of the target consumers. Gwalior Suitings uses Nawab of Pataudi for promoting its suitings, to project an image of class and exclusivity and perceives that this image

would match well with the self-concept of their target consumers.

- **Learning and Memory:** Everyday we are exposed to a wide and diverse range of information. But we can barely recall a small fraction of it the next day. We only remember that which is of relevance and importance to us, or where we have a motivation to remember. Consider a situation where a family is viewing a TV programme and the accompanying advertisements. Out of the 15-20 advertisements, the seven year old daughter may remember the advertisement for Barbie dolls, the husband (who drives the car) may remember the advertisement of radial car tyres and the wife may remember the advertisement for a new model of mixer-grinder. This is because each one of them has a motivation for different products. Our motives, attitudes and personality act as filters by letting in only relevant information and keeping all other information out. Surely we would see the product, hear its jingle on the radio but chances are it will not register in our minds. We will remember it only for a short while and then forget it This is known as selective retention. We retain in our memories only selective information.
- **Information Processing:** This refers to the process and activities which consumers engage in while gathering, assimilating and evaluating information. The manner in which we assimilate and evaluate this selective information is determined by our motives, attitudes and personality and self-concept. Thus,the same information may be evaluated in a different manner by two different individuals and the ensuing response may also be very different. A half-filled glass elicits the response "a half-empty glass from, one consumer while another reacts by saying it is "half-full".

Variable of External Environment

- **Cultural Influences:** The first of the influences is that of cultural variables. Culture is defined as the complex, sum total of knowledge, belief, traditions, customs, art, morals, law and any other habits acquired by people as members of a society. Culture of one society differs from that of another. Many of our actions, and behaviour as consumers stem from our cultural background for instance, the emphasis on saving schemes oriented towards saving for a daughter's marriage or the preferred attitude towards gold as a form of saving are the result of our unique cultural influence.
- **Sub-cultural Influences:** Within a given culture, there are many groups or segments of people with distinct customs, tradition and behaviour,

which set them apart from other people. All Indians share one common cultural heritage, but the Hindu Brahmins of Tamil Nadu are very different from the Hindu Bengalis of Calcutta in the same way as Kashmiri Hindus are different from the Hindus of Gujarat. Each of these people, within one cultural mainstream, have uniquely distinct sub-cultures. They have their style of dress, food habits, religious traditions and rites all of which have implication for the marketer. Sumeet Mixer and Grinder developed special heavy duty motor to withstand continuous running required for grinding rice for dosa, vada, idli—staple food items of the South Indian cuisine. Similarly, marketers of spices need to modulate taste and formulation according to the consumers taste, which varies from state to state.

- **Social Class Influences:** Social class is a group consisting of a number of people who share more or less equal position in a society. Within a social class people tend to share same values, beliefs, and exhibit similar patterns of behaviour and consumption. Some social classes are ranked as higher and lower. Social classes differ from one society to another, and their standing in society may also change over time. Social classes may be defined by parameters such as income and occupation. The belongingness to a social class influence decisions such as choice of residence, type of holiday, means of entertainment and leisure.
- **Social Group Influences:** A social group is a collection of individuals who share some common attitudes and a sense of relationship as a result of interaction with each other. Social groups may be primary where face-to-face interaction take place frequently, such as families, work groups, and study groups. Secondly groups are those where the relationship is a more formalized and less personal in nature.
- **Family Influences:** Family is a social group which can be defined as a primary group. It needs to be studied in great detail as it is one of the strongest sources of influences on consumer behavior. The first and strongest influence on a child is that of his family and he imbibes many behavioral patterns from other family members subconsciously and these tend to stay with him even after attaining adulthood. Further, within a family many decisions are made jointly with various members exerting different degree of influence. The changing structure of families as the joint family system gradually gives way to single nucleus families also influence the consumer behavior.
- **Personal Influences:** Each individual is influenced by the family, social class, sub-cultural and cultural group to which he belongs, and

yet has his own distinct personality which influences his decisions and behavior as a consumer. The probability of trying a new product or a new brand will depend on the type of personality of the consumer. The process of evaluation of different products and different brands will vary from person to person. For one, price may be the most important parameter in making the decision to buy a water geyser, for another it is convenience, and for yet another it may be the status symbol value.

Q2. Who is a consumer? Describe the nature of consumer behaviour.

Ans. Consumer is a broad label for any individual or household that use goods and services generated within the economy. The concept of a consumer occurs in different contexts, so that the usage and significance of the term may vary. The 'consumer' is the one who consumes the goods and services produced. As such, consumers plays a vital role in the economic system of a nation because in the absence of the effective demand that emanates from them, the economy virtually collapses. Mahatma Gandhi said a customer is the most important visitor in our premises. He is not dependent on us, we are on him. He is not an interruption to our work, he is the purpose of it.Typically when business people and economists talk of consumers they are talking about person as consumer, an aggregated commodity item with little individuality other than that expressed in the buy/not-buy decision. However,there is a trend in marketing to individualize the concept. Instead of generating broad demographic profiles and psycho-graphic profiles of market segments, marketers have started to engage in personalized marketing, permission marketing, and mass customization.

Consumer behaviour can be defined as: "The decision process and physical activity engaged in when evaluating, acquiring, using or disposing of goods and services." This definition raises a few queries in our minds—What or who are consumers? What is the decision process that they engage in? Answers to these questions help define the broad nature of consumer behaviour.

Q3. Describe the decision process and physical activities, preceding the purchase undertaken by various members of the family.

Ans. The physical activity which we focus upon in the course of consumer behaviour is that of making the purchase. But there are a number of influences affecting the purchase and a number of individuals may be involved in exerting these influences. So the purchase action that is visible to us maybe the result of a interplay of a number of complex and hidden variables which may have influenced the ultimate purchase activity. The final purchase is just one activity in the entire series of physical and mental activities that may have occurred in this whole process. Some of these activities may precede the purchase while others may take place later. But because all these activities exert influence on the purchase they are considered a part of consumer behaviour, more specifically a part of the decision process.

Take an example of a father, we call Mr. Verma. buying a TV for his family. It is possible that the consumer behaviour involving mental processes and activities may have taken place in the following sequence and manner. Mr. Verma's teenage daughter, sees a new colour TV at her friend's house. She then raises the issue of buying a colour TV to replace then existing black and white TV. The family discusses the issue and agrees that it is indeed time they bought a colour TV. The next day Mr. Verma discusses the matter with his friend and colleague, Mr. Mohan. He visits Mr. Mohan's home to see for himself the quality of the EC colour TV that he has. Mrs. Verma also finds out more about the various brands, prices and quality of different brands, from her sister who recently purchased a colour TV. Her sister has a Crown TV and recommends the same. Meanwhile Mr. Verma's daughter checks out the brands of TVs that her various friends have at their respective homes and concludes that BPL is the best. In the next few days the entire Verma family makes it a point to carefully study any advertisements of colour TV that appear in the newspaper, magazine or TV. At all social occasions they raise the question of which is the best colour TV to buy amongst their friends and relatives and mentally, mark the different positive and negative points of different brands. Within two weeks the Vermas have collected enough information to take a decision to buy BPL, but they need more specific information. So one evening they visit two dealer outlets in their neighbourhood market to find out more about prices. They find that the BPL TV is rather expensive and beyond their budget. So they settle for Crown which was recommended by quite a few of their friends and the price is affordable too. Moreover, the dealer offered them a special five per cent discount and a free antenna alongwith free installation. The information that this company would soon he offering a VCR at a reasonable price clinched the decision in favouur of Crown.

The activity and thought process which resulted in the final purchase of TV started well before the actual purchase took place and was spread over a period of two to three weeks. This entire process forms part of consumer behaviour.

Depending on the nature of product or service in question, the mental decision process accompanying the physical act of purchase may vary from very simple to extremely complex, and from being instantaneous in nature to time consuming and elabouuurate. But they all constitute consumer behaviour. Thus, not only the overt, observable physical behaviour exhibited in the art of making a purchase, but all the accompanying, preceding and following mental processes and activities also are an integral part of consumer behaviour.

In case of the stock of regular brands of toilet soap being depleted at home, its purchase needs no elabouuurate decision process or activity of comparison and evaluation. Rather the purchase decision is almost an automatic one.

Q4. Define the process of consumer dicision-making.

Ans. Consumer behaviour was a relatively new field of study in the mid-to late-1960s. Because it had no history or body of research of its own, marketing theorists borrowed heavily from concepts developed in other scientific disciplines, such as *psychology* (the study of the individual), *sociology* (the study of groups), *social psychology* (the study of how an individual operates in groups), *anthropology* (the influence of society on the individual), and *economics* to form the basis of this new marketing discipline. Many early theories concerning consumer behaviour were based on economic theory, on the notion that individuals act rationally to maximize their benefits (satisfactions) in the purchase of goods and services. Later research discovered that consumers are just as likely to purchase impulsively and to be influenced not only by family and friends, by advertisers and role models, but also by mood, situation, and emotion. All of these factors combine to form a comprehensive model of consumer behaviour that reflects both the cognitive and emotional aspects of consumer decision-making.

The process of consumer decision-making can be viewed as three distinct but interlocking stages: the input stage, the process stage, and the output stage.

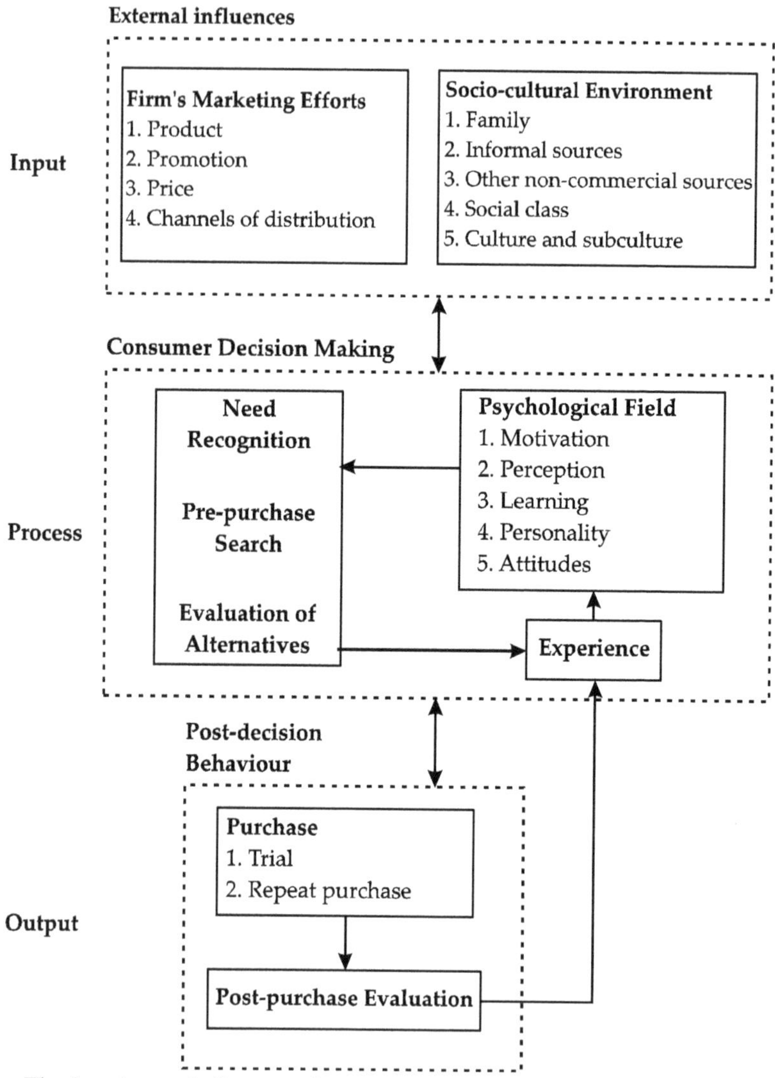

The *input* stage influences the consumer's recognition of a product need and consists of two major sources of information: the firm's marketing efforts (the product itself, its price, its promotion, and where it is sold) and the external sociological influences on the consumer (family, friends, neighbours, other informal and non-commercial sources, social class, and cultural and subcultural memberships). The cumulative impact of each firm's marketing efforts, the influence of family, friends, and neighbours, and society's existing code of behaviour are all inputs that are likely to affect what consumers purchase and how they use what they buy.

The *process* stage of the model focuses on how consumers make decisions. The psychological factors inherent in each individual (motivation, perception, learning, personality, and attitudes) affect how the external inputs from the input stage influence the consumer's recognition of a need, prepurchase search for information, and evaluation of alternatives. The experience gained through evaluation of alternatives, in turn, affects the consumer's existing psychological attributes.

The *output* stage of the consumer decision-making model consists of two closely related post decision activities: purchase behaviour and post purchase evaluation. Purchase manufacturer's coupon and may actually by a trial purchase; if the consumer is satisfied, he or she may repeat the purchase. The trial is the exploratory phase of purchase behaviour in which the consumer evaluates the product through direct use. A repeat purchase usually signifies product adoption. For a relatively durable product such as a laptop the purchase is more likely to signify adoption.

Q5. Discuss the applications of consumer behaviour in the field of marketing.

Ans. Marketing is defined as "human activity directed at satisfying needs and wants through exchange processes". Thus,the beginning of marketing lies in identifying unsatisfied human needs and wants and understanding the ensuing activity which people engage in to fulfil these. And that is the realm of consumer behaviour. Consumer behaviour and marketing go hand-in-hand. Trying to do the latter without an understanding of the former in akin to firing a shot in the dark. Consumer behaviour has a number of application in the area of marketing.

Fig. 1.1: Consumer Behavior

- **Analysing Market Opportunity:** behaviour's study consumer behaviour helps in identifying needs and wants which are unfulfilled.

This is done by examining trends in income, consumers lifestyles, and emerging influences. The trend towards increasing number of working wives, and greater emphasis on leisure and convenience have signalled the emerging needs for household gadgets such as vacuum cleaner, washing machine, and mixer grinder. Tortoise Mosquito repellant coils and Good Knight electrical repellants were marketed in response to a genuinely felt need of the people.

- **Selecting the Target Market:** with the help of consumer trends would reveal distinct groups of consumers with very distinct needs and wants. Knowing who these groups are, how they behave, how they decide to buy enables the marketer to market products/services especially suited to their needs. All this is made possible only by studying in depth the consumer and his purchase behaviour.

  A study of potential consumers for shampoo revealed that there was a class of consumers who would like to use shampoo only on special occasions and who otherwise use soap to wash their hair. Further, this consumer class would not afford to spend more than three or four rupees on shampoo. Having identified this target market, companies with leading brands launched their shampoos in small sachets containing enough quantity for one wash and priced just at two or three rupees.
- **Determining the Product Mix:** Having identified the unfulfilled need slot and having modified the product to suit differing consumer tastes, the marketer now has to get down to the brass tacks of marketing. He has to determine the right mix of product, price, promotion, and advertising. Again consumer behaviour is extremely useful as it helps find answers to many perplexing questions.
- **Use in Non-profit and Social Marketing:** The knowledge of consumer behaviour is also useful in the marketing of non-profit or social or governmental services of institution such as hospitals, voluntary agencies, law enforcement, and tax collection agencies. The income tax authorities have always been perceived in negative manner by the common man who fears them and views them in a suspicious light. To overcome this poor image, advertisements on TV and in newspapers and magazines are regularly released, wherein a friendly, helpful image is sought to be projected. Moreover, there is greater dissemination of information regarding the rights and responsibilities of the taxpayer. Similarly, Delhi Police is trying to overcome the problem of poor image by projecting itself as always alert and available for help through regular newspaper advertisements.

Q6. What is lifestyle marketing? Describe its demographic, psychographic, aspects.

Ans. Lifestyle marketing is a process of establishing relationships between products offered in the market and targeted lifestyle groups. It involves segmenting the market on the basis of lifestyle dimensions, positioning the product in a way that appeals to the activities, interests and opinions of the targeted market and undertaking specific promotional campaigns which exploit lifestyle appeals to enhance the market value of the offered product. Lifestyle is "a distinctive mode of behaviour centred around activities, interests, opinions, attitudes and demographic characteristics distinguishing one segment of a population from another. A consumer's lifestyle is seen as the sum of his interactions with his environment. Lifestyle studies are a component of the broader behavioural concept called psychographics."

Demographic variables help marketers "locate" their target market and psychographic variables provide the marketer with more insight about the segment. Psychographics is, in common parlance, lifestyle analysis or AIO research. In its most widely practiced form, a psychographic study consists of a long list of statement designed to capture relevant aspects of a consumer, like personality, hinting motives, interests, attitudes, beliefs, and values. When the study becomes oriented towards a particular product, the consumers have to respond to statements which are selected for the purpose, i.e. on products, brands, services, competitive situations, etc.

The demographic and psychographic lifestyle approaches are highly complimentary and work best together. People hailing from the same sub-culture, social class and even occupation follow quite different lifestyles. If we can create a fictitious Mrs. Kapoor to look at possibly it may be like this; She may choose to live a "belonging" lifestyle which will be reflected in her wearing conservative clothes, spending considerable time with her family and participating in social activities. Or she can be an "achiever" marked by an active personal life and playing hard when it comes to travel and sports. It can be seen that lifestyle depicts the "whole person" in active interaction with his environment.

The lifestyle analysis adds a great amount of understanding to a typical demographic description. A person buying a new designer shirt may be 34 years old, married and living in a three bedroom house and having two children. The lifestyle analysis would help marketers to paint a more human portrait to their target market.

Q7. Differentiate between Psychological and Psychographic market segmentations.

Ans. Market segmentation can be defined as the process of dividing a market into distinct subsets of consumers with common needs or characteristics and selecting one or more segments to target with a distinct marketing mix. Before the widespread acceptance of market segmentation, the prevailing way of doing business with consumers was through mass marketing — that is, offering the same product and marketing mix to all consumers.

- **Psychological Segmentation:** Psychological characteristics refer to the inner or intrinsic qualities of the individual consumer. Consumer segmentation strategies are often based on specific psychological variables. For instance, consumers may be segmented in terms of their motivations, personality, perceptions, learning, and attitudes.
- **Psychographic Segmentation:** Marketing practitioners have heartily embraced psychographic research, which is closely aligned with psychological research, especially personality and attitude measurement. This form of applied consumer research has proven to be a valuable marketing tool that helps identify promising consumer segments that are likely to be responsive to specific marketing messages. The psychographic profile of a consumer segment can be thought of as a composite of consumers' measured activities, interests, and opinions (AIOs). As an approach to constructing consumer psychographic profiles, AIO research seeks consumers' responses to a large number of statements that measure *activities* (how the consumer or family spends time, e.g. camping, volunteering at a local hospital, going to baseball games), *interests* (the consumer's or family's preferences and priorities, *e.g.* home fashion, food), and *opinions* (how the consumer feels about a wide variety of events and political issues, social issues, the state of the economy, ecology). In their most common form, AIO-psychographic studies use a battery of statements (a psychographic inventory) designed to identify relevant aspects of a consumer's personality, buying motives, interests, attitudes, beliefs, and values.

  AIO research has even been employed to explore pet ownership as a segmentation base. One study has found that people who do *not* have pets are more conservative in nature, more brand loyal, and more likely to agree with statements such as "I am very good at managing money" and "It is important for me to look well dressed." Such findings can be used by marketers when developing promotional messages for their products and services.

Q8. Describe the Values and Lifestyle classification.

Ans. The VALS system of classification classifies adults (18+) in the US into distinctive lifestyle groups. Each group is based on inner psychological needs (values) and behaviour response patterns (lifestyles) which their values predict. The psychological theory used in VALS draws heavily on Abraham Maslow's Hierarchy on Needs. The VALS theory and database were first applied to markets in 1978. VALS provides a dynamic framework of values and lifestyles which helps to explain why people act as they do as social groups and as consumers. VALS, unlike some other approaches, waves together: 1. Demographics, 2. Attitudes, 3. Activities, 4. Consumption patterns, 5. Brand preferences, 6. Media graphics.

The VALS study leads to the identification of four major groups, i.e. the need driven (the poor and uneducated), the outer directed (the middle or upper income class consumer whose lifestyle is directed by external criteria), and the inner directed (people who are motivated more by inner needs than by the expectations of others). The fourth segment, called integrated represents individuals who have been able to combine the best of both outer directed and inner directed values.

Among the need driven there are survivors and sustainers. In the case of survivors, the purchase motivation is found to be price dominant. They are also not very knowledgeable shoppers. The sustainers are motivated by brand names, guarantees and are generally impulse buyers. The outer directed belongers go for proven popularity of products. They are brand loyal and careful shoppers. The outer directed emulators buy products to impress other people and use products to announce status. The achievers buy high tech items. They want original, top of the line products. They are brand conscious and very loyal. The inner directed I-AM-ME's go after fads and do not mind being *avant garde*. The inner directed experimental buy products for the sake of experimenting. They get tremendous amount of satisfaction from the purchase process itself. The inner directed societally conscious customer wants value for money. He is a simple, frugal person, who seeks information and reads labels carefully.

Q9. Write down the characteristics & influences of lifestyle.

Ans. Feldman and Theilbar describe lifestyle by the following characteristics:

(1) Lifestyle is a group phenomenon: A person's lifestyle bears the influence of his/her participation in social groups and of his/her relationships with others. Two clerks in the same office may exhibit different lifestyles.

(2) Lifestyle pervades various aspects of life: An individual's lifestyle may result in certain consistency of behaviour. Knowing a person's conduct in one aspect of life may enable us to predict how he/she may behave in other areas.

(3) Lifestyle implies a central life interest: For every individual there are many central life interests like family, work, leisure, sexual exploits, religion, politics, etc. that may fashion his interaction with the environment.

(4) Lifestyles vary according to sociologically relevant variables: The rate of social change in a society has a great deal to do with variations in lifestyles. So do age, sex, religion, ethnicity, and social class. The increase in the number of double income families and that of working women have resulted in completely different lifestyles in the 1980s in India.

Q10. What are the influences on lifestyle?

Ans. Cultural and societal variables establish the outer boundaries of lifestyle specific to our culture. The interaction of group and individual expectations and values creates a systematic pattern of behaviour. This is the lifestyle pattern that determines purchase decisions. When goods and services available in the market are in tune with lifestyle patterns and values, consumer market reactions are favouurable. And purchases that reinforce these patterns further illuminate these lifestyles. Lazer's lifestyle hierarchy brings out these interactions.

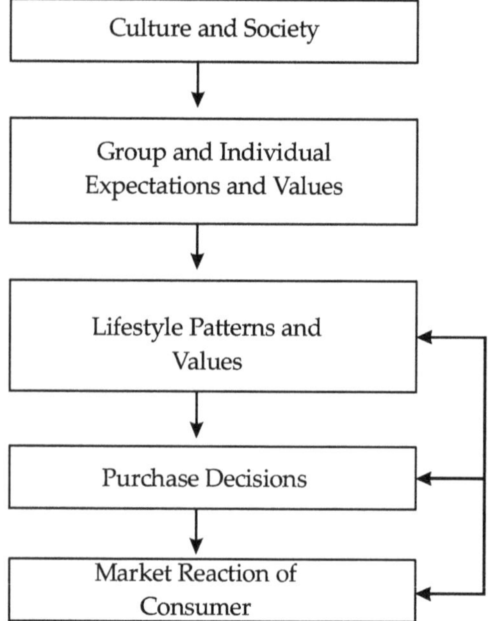

Fig. 1.2: Hierarchy of Influences on Lifestyles

Q11. What are the approaches to study lifestyle?

Or

Discuss any two approaches to study lifestyle of a consumer.

Or

Write a short note on AIO Inventories and their use.

Ans. The study of lifestyle is interdisciplinary. It draws on a variety of disciplines such as anthropology, psychology, sociology, and economics. Marketing uses this eclectic approach for segmenting, targeting, and positioning which forms the core of marketing strategy. Because lifestyle refers to the way in which people live and spend money, consumers psychographic profiles are derived by measuring different aspects of consumer behaviour such as:

- Products and services consumed,
- Activities, interests and opinions,
- Value systems,
- Personality traits and self-conception ,
- Attitude towards various product classes.

Many approaches are available to the study of psychographic variables. One of the ways is to study the lifestyle variables by an AIO inventory for use in segmenting, targeting, and positioning. Another lifestyle approach is by using VALS typology.

In constructing an inventory of such lifestyle statements researchers first go through market research studies that might be of help in isolating psychographic variables. Motivation research studies which reveal consumer's reflections on their experiences and needs are a good source. Based on such reviews psychographic statements are prepared which bring out the range of activities, interest and opinions that the researcher wishes to evaluate. In constructing a psychographic inventory, it has to be thoroughly assessed whether consumers will understand the meaning of the each of the statements as the marketer expected them to be interpreted. It is also important to avoid statements that lead consumers to make a socially acceptable response which really does not reflect their true feelings or likely ways of interaction with environment. In responding to an inventory as explained above consumers are usually asked to rate in a quantifiable rating scale as is used in marketing research studies, the extent of their agreement or disagreement with each statement and results are statistically evaluated. Thus,psychographic research produces quantifiable insights that are usually presented in tabular format. The measurement is similar to the measurement of personality traits in that it requires the use of self-administered questionnaire or inventories.

Q12. Discuss the various application of AIO studies.

Ans. Studying the lifestyle closely through the AIO inventory of heavy/ medium/light users of a product has been found to be immensely useful for marketers. In the US studies have been done regarding the heavy use of beer, eye make-up and bank credit cards. When it was revealed that 23% of the people who drink beer consume 80% of the beverage sold, the heavy beer user became the advertising target of the new campaign. Willian Wells and Douglas Tigert used an AIO inventory to probe the heavy user of eye cosmetics. Demographic data revealed that such women were young, well educated and metropolitan. But she also tended to. be a heavy smoker and more inclined than the average woman to make long distance telephone calls. From the responses to statements, she emerged as one who fantasises about trips around the world, and as one who wanted a very stylish home.

In a study Plummer applied to bank credit card users, males who used bank charge cards heavily were described as urbane and active with high income level and occupational and educational achievements. The heavy card user places high value on personal appearance consistent with his career and lifestyle. He was found to buy at least three new suits a year, to belong to several organisations and revealed contemporary attitudes and opinions.

Thus, a study of personality, lifestyle and social class gives a more comprehensive consumer profile and not a mere physical description of demographics.

Female Lifestyle Types

- **Cathy the contented housewife (Beena Ganguly in the Dalda Refined Oil advertisements.** Cathy epitomises simplicity. She is devoted to her family and faithfully serves them as mother housewife and cook. She enjoys a relaxed pace and avoids anything which might disturb her equilibrium.
- **Candice—the chic subarbanite (Kitu Gidwani in the Halo Shampoo advertisement).** Candice is an urban woman. She is well educated and genteel. Socialising is an important part of her life. She is a doer, interested in sports and the outdoors, politics and current affairs. Her life is hectic and lived at a fast clip. She is a voracious reader and there are few magazines she does not read.
- **Eleanor—the elegant socialite (Shyamolie Verma in the Lakme advertisement).** Eleanor is a woman with style. She lives in the city because that is where she want to be. She likes the socio-economic aspects of the city in terms of her career and leisure time activities. She is fashion conscious and dresses well. She is financially secure

and Hence,not a careful shopper. She shops for status and style and not for price. She is a cosmopolitan woman who has travelled abroad and wants to.

- **Mildred—the militant mother (As an exercise, can you think of an example so as to draw a comparison).** Mildred is a woman who got married young and had children before she was ready to raise a family. Now she is unhappy. She is frustrated and vents her frustration by rebelling against the system. Television provides an ideal medium for her to live out her fantasies.
- **Thelma—the old fashioned traditionalist (Lalitaji of the Surf advertisement).** Thelma is a lady who has lived a good life. She has been a devoted wife, a doting mother, and a conscientious housewife. Even now, when most of her children have left home, her life is centred around the kitchen. She lacks higher education and has little appreciation for the arts or cultural activities. Her spare time is spent watching TV.

To make these distilled profiles even more useful for segmenting markets for specific products aimed at women, the researchers then portrayed these segments in terms of an index of product usage.

Combining these various pieces of information we can infer that Thelma—the traditionalist is most likely to use hair colouring, but least likely to use make-up. In contrast a marketer of a leading line of cosmetics, say Lakme in India is likely to prefer a target women like Eleanor. Such women are predisposed to using cologne, lipstick, hairspray, nailpolish and various other forms of expensive make-up.

Male Lifestyle Types are:

- Ben—the self-made businessman (Reminiscent of Gavaskar in Dinesh advertisement.)
- Scott—the successful professional (Shekhar Kapur in the Digjam advertisement).
- Dale—the devoted family man (Zafer Lalji in the Cadbury advertisement).
- Fred—the frustrated factory worker (Ramu in the Nirodh advertisement).
- Herman—the retiring homebody (Dadaji in the Dabur Chyavanprash advertisement).

Q13. What are the applications of lifestyled marketing?

Ans. The most striking uses of lifestyle concept and allied research have been made in positioning of new products, repositioning of existing products, developing new product concepts, and creating new product opportunities in specific fields. In congruence to the product concept chosen, lifestyle research is utilised for selecting media, formulating media and promotion strategies and improving retail performance. Lifestyle concept is also utilised as a framework for presenting research recommendations, since it is capable of offering to the marketers, potraits of target group expressed in an uncomplicated manner.

Repositioning an Old/Existing Product: Sometimes existing products may sell well below their forecast potential or the company may discover a new, more profitable niche, nearer to the core market where it may now want to position the product. Repositioning is often a contingency planned for in the new product development process, primarily as a remedial measure. Generally in markets where the competitive activity is high, the need while positioning the product for the fixed time is to get a foot hold in the market. After gaining market penetration, establishing distribution and creating a certain degree of market acceptability, the manufacturer may, through repositioning, or a series of repositionings move the product closer to the core market. Lifestyle marketing strategies help considerably in reducing the amount of 'market grouping' that repositioning may entail.

Positioning of New Products: Positioning comprises finding the most profitable niche for a new product in terms of target market. Lifestyle research, for example, an AIO portrait, of heavy users for any given consumer product not only tells us how old they are, where they live and to what socio-economic group they belong, it also tells us what products are they likely to buy, what their interests and opinions are. This provides an unusually rich body of data for use in marketing decisions related to the positioning of a new product. Decisions concerning the precise target group at which the product is to be aimed, the product image to be designed, the media vehicle and the type of promotion strategy to be taken so that the complete product package is in conformity with a particular lifestyle/styles.

Creating Promotional Strategies: Lifestyle information is helpful in developing promotional strategies in a number of ways. It gives the decision-maker a much more complete profile of the type of consumer who will be at the receiving end of the communication. Lifestyle data suggests the style of language, the tone of voice and even the appeal that may be Utilised to reach that kind of consumer. Further, lifestyle information indicates how the product or service fits into people's lives, how they feel about it and how they may be using the product or service to communicate with others. This information can be Utilised by the marketer to decide upon the kind of image he wants to imbue the product with.

The Indian marketing scenario, especially for consumer durables, is becoming fiercely competitive. Hence,companies are realising that merely highlighting the attributes of their product or of the company in terms of demographic or geographic dimensions is not enough to be successful in the market place. Marketers have come to appreciate that buying behaviour is influenced by the consumer's lifestyle. Companies dealing in cosmetics, apparel, packaged food, etc. are seeking opportunities in lifestyle segmentation. Stores, especially those dealing in apparel, have started keeping merchandise which goes with a particular lifestyle. The Bata-Northstar advertisement aiming at the "Young, western oriented, fun loving crowd" is an example of this approach. Further, the fact that Bata Ltd. has expanded its product range to and also a full range of active sports wear under "Power", bring out their attempt at lifestyle marketing. The growing westernization of youth in India and the resulting change in lifestyle is responsible for the ever increasing demand for jeans in the country. Denim as a lifestyle-fabric is fast gaining acceptance in India, transcending demographic segments and marketers are making use of this phenomenon.

Developing New Product Concepts: Study of existing market segments and analysis of their needs have typically been used to conceptualise on new product opportunities. Traditionally, demographic segmentation, or standard consumer classification of major groups like the educated youth, the young collegiate, the urban housewife, etc. have been used to define and study the segments. Lifestyle studies on the other hand can be used to complement the demographic studies in terms of market needs, customer and non-customer attitudes, the opinions related to product usage and the interests of the target customers, to be able to define the product attributes which may be congenial to certain lifestyles. For example users of fluoride toothpaste may have different expectations from it. Some use it as a medicinal aid to oral hygiene; others feel it should give cosmetic benefit. Even among these who use it as a medicine, there are two sets of expectations, some believing that a medicine ought to taste like a medicine while others strongly feel that just because the fluoride toothpaste has a medicinal ingredient, it need not taste like one. In developing the concept of a new fluoride toothpaste, you will find that a complete inventory of Attitudes, Interests, and Opinions of the consumers will help you in defining the attributes of the final product, as you can define the requirements of the different lifestyle segment and then conceptualize as to which segment you wish to aim the product at.

Q14. What is organizational buying behaviour?

Ans. Organisational buying is a complex process of decision-making and communication, which takes place over time, involving several organisational members and relationship with other firms and institutions. Further, it is much more than a simple act of placing an order with the suppliers. In this sense, we can define organisational buying behaviour as the decision-making process by which formal organisations establish the need for purchased products and services and identify, evaluate and choose among alternative brands and suppliers.

It is important here to recognise the emphasis on the *decision process* rather than on a single act of placing an order. The case of the desert cooler clearly brings out the process which began with identification of the need to finally placing of an order. Based on several observations of buying situation, we can identified this process as comprising eight steps of this decision process:

- Need recognition.
- Definition of the characteristics and quantity of item needed.
- Development of the specifications to guide the procurement.
- Search for and qualification of potential sources.
- Acquisition and analysis of proposals.
- Evaluation of proposals and selection of suppliers.
- Selection of an order routine.
- Performance feedback and evaluation.

Q15. Identify some typical characteristics of organizational buying behaviour.

Or

Explain the major influences on organizatioinal buying.

Ans. Some of these typical characteristics are described below:

(1) Organisational buying is a multiperson buying activity: A large number of buying situations in organisations (manufacturing, government, hospitals, educational institutions) would involve many persons. These persons may be from different functions (production, purchase, design, maintenance), may have different backgrounds (engineers, MBA, graduates, etc.) may have different hierarchical levels within the organisation (Managing Director, General Manager, Material Manager). Further, persons in a buying situation, may appear to play different roles over the entire buying decision exercise. A grand conceptualisation of various roles of the different members is the concept of the *Buying Centre*. The various members of the buying centre may appear to play any of the following roles:

- **Users** like production department person.
- **Influencers** like Managing Director, Design Engineers or Consultants.
- **Deciders** like the committee appointed by Pragati Enterprises.
- **Buyers** like the people from the purchase or materials department.
- **Gatekeepers** like those who can control the flow of information within an organisation.
- **Specifiers** like consultants or design or production people who may develop the specifications of the product or services needed.

The concept of Buying Centre is a very useful conceptualisation and it can help immensely in developing effective marketing strategies.

(2) It is a formal activity which follows the procedures laid down in an organisation: Irrespective of the rupee value of technical complexities of products and services, buying activities have to conform to the formal process and procedures of an organisation. Even for emergencies, a typical organisation would have a set of policies, and it is imperative for the suppliers to be aware of these. Further, all buying decisions are finally converted into formal contracts between buyers and suppliers.

(3) Longer time lag between efforts and results: Due to multiperson and a formal activity, the organisation buying decisions take typically longer time. This leads to greater time lags between the application of the market effort and obtaining of the buying response. A marketer may develop unrealistic plans if he is unaware of the response time of his customer for various buying situations.

(4) Rational but also emotional activity: In spite of a formal activity following a rational criteria of evaluation, organisational buying cannot be devoid of the emotional (or irrational) aspects. This is because it involves human beings in the buying decisions. These human considerations are likely to play vital role in situations of almost similar alternatives or similar choices—like buying of commodities, raw materials, standard products and components, etc-etc.

(5) The uniqueness of organisations: In spite of the above common characteristics, no two organisations would be similar in their buying behaviour and decisions. These differences would be due to the nature of buying problems, objectives, resources, capabilities and so on. It is Therefore,important to consider each organisation as a separate segment at the selling level.

Q16. Who are the organisational customers?

Ans. By now, we must be wondering about this 'ghost': organisational customer. Perhaps we need to become more clear about the constituents of the 'organisational' markets. Conceptually, anyone besides the 'household' customer, i.e. those customers who are buying for self, can be valid cases of organisational customers. However, a useful and comprehensive way to identify the organisational customers is to visualise the entire chain of the participants who may be involved in the production and marketing of goods and services. Thus,for a desert cooler, the manufacturer may need galvanised iron sheets for body, angle iron for frames, wood shavings for water pads, exhaust fan for air and so on. Similarly, each supplier of the needed items would also need the down stream products in form of raw material, components and parts. Thus, an exhaust fan manufacturer would need cold rolled strips for fan blades, silicon iron laminations for rotor of the motor, wires for coils, and so on. The chain, as we would begin to see, is long. Similarly, in order to market, there would be a need of distributors and retailers. This organizational customer can have several types and forms:

- **Mining and Extractive Industries:** Coal India Limited, ONGC, Hindustan Copper Limited are some examples.
- **Material Processing Industries:** Tata Steel, Steel Authority of India Limited (SAIL), Bharat Aluminium Corporation (BALCO) are some examples.
- **Manufacturing of Parts and Assembly:** Bharat Forge, MICO, Sundaram Clayton, Semiconductors of India Limited, GEC, Larsen & Toubro are some amongst a very large number of part and assembly manufacturers catering to a variety of needs.
- **Final Assembly:** Desert Cooler Manufacturer (there are several local brands), T.V. manufacturers (Onida, Weston, Nelco), Truck manufacturers (TELCO, Ashok Leyland) and the like are some examples. Like components and parts manufacturers, there could be many assembly units for numerous end products.
- **Distributors:** These could be several for each product like bearings, tubes, steel, electrical appliances and so on.

Perhaps, it is now easy for us to recognise that the area of operation of what we call as "organisational marketing" is very vast and heterogenous. In such a scenario, a legitimate question would be the validity of generalisations in form of 'typical characteristics'. Thus, from the viewpoint of practice, it is imperative to study the organisational buying behaviour for the specific product-market situation.

A second way to identify the organisational customers is to classify them into three categories. Industrial (all manufacturing organisations), Institutional (service organisations like universities, hospitals, hotels, distribution firms) and government (CPWD, DGS&D, Defence and so on).

Besides the ownership pattern (public, private, government) and type of business (manufacturing, service) it is important to remember that it is neither the size (big, medium, or small) nor the products, which separates organisational customers from household customers.

Q17. What influences organizational buying? Try to analyse the main influence–environmental, organizational, interpersonal, or personal.

Or

Discuss the major influences on Organizational Buying.

Ans. A segment of economists and marketers believe that the dominant influences are essentially economic. Lowest price or lowest cost are Thus,considered as the only criteria to select suppliers. On the other hand a few take another extreme view of declaring all organisational buying as an emotional or non-rational act as it involves human beings making it difficult to maintain rationality or objectivity. Accordingly, some suppliers feel that with strong personal relationships or with the ability to win over the purchases through lures and personal attractions, they may get preference over others. Both the viewpoints are the two extremes and reflect only a limited view of the reality. What perhaps is needed is a balanced viewpoint recognising that organisational customers respond to both economic and personal factors. Where there is a close similarity in supplier offers; organisational customers have little basis for only economic criterion. Since any brand of desired product could meet the organisational objective, personal factors played an important role. On the other hand, where competing products/brands differ substantially, organisational customers may pay more attention to the economic considerations.

A comprehensive view of influences has been provided be Webster and Wind. They have grouped the various influences into four areas: environmental, organisational, interpersonal, and individual.

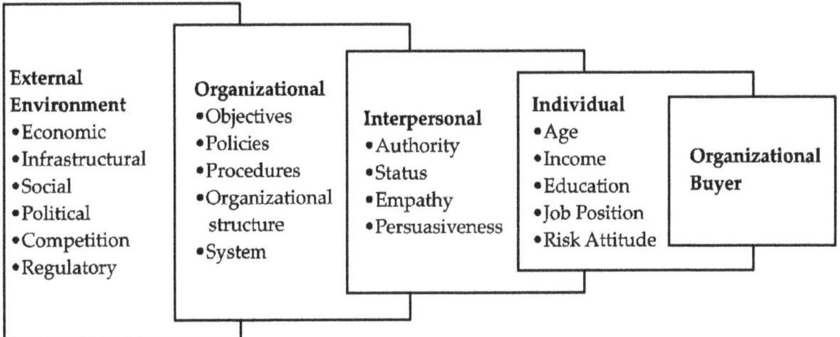

Fig. 1.3: Major Influences on Organisational Buying Behaviour

(1) Environmental Factors: These factors include economical, political, technical, legal or regulatory, technological, infrastructural and cultural factors. Environmental factors interact with each other to produce information, values, norms and general business conditions. The influence of environmental factors can be pervasive. A handy Indian example is that of credit squeeze announced by the commercial banks around 1975 against inventory holdings. This was based on Tandon Committee Report on the management of working capital by the firms. This single change in the environment, i.e. credit squeeze on inventories had a salutory affect on organisational buying behaviour and led to major structural and procedural changes in the buying behaviour of industrial customers.

Similarly the persistent power shortages in some States in India have prevented the use of sophisticated automatic elevators in the office and residential buildings and in spite of the availability, the preference is still for manually operated elevators with shutter type of doors.

An industrial marketer should be aware of the environmental factors which may affect the buyer behaviour and correspondingly fine tune its marketing strategy. Failure to recognize the influences may lead to wasteful efforts.

(2) Organisational Factors: While discussing the characteristics of organisational buying behaviour, it was mentioned that organisations may differ from each other due to objectives, procedures, organisational structure, systems and technology: It is important to recognise the influence of such organisational factors on the buying behaviour. A study by Sarin on four very large industrial organisations in India revealed major changes in the buying structures and systems of the Indian firms. Some of these were:

- Innovativeness in Organisational Buying.
- Emergence of "Buyer" as an Important Member of the Buying Centre.
- Decentralization and Centralization of Materials.
- Computerization of Organisational Buying.
- Separate Buying for Specialized Jobs.
- Concern to Prevent Unhealthy Transactions between Buyers and Marketers.
- Recognition at the Top Level.

(3) The Interpersonal Factors: Organisational buying is a multi-person activity. The concept of buying centre highlights the roles which different members of the buying organisation may play in the entire buying decision-making exercise. The situation becomes more complex due to different statuses, authority, empathy and persuasiveness of the members of the buying centre. These may lead to conflicts. Though difficult, but an organisational marketer may make, attempts to become familiar with the internal dynamics of the buying process within a customer organisation. Sheth has identified four ways which organisations use for conflict resolutions:

- **Problem Solving Approach:** It involves information acquisition and deliberation for more time.
- **Persuasion:** Attempt is made to influence the opinions of dissenting members by asking them to reduce the importance of the criteria they are using in favouur of better overall achievements of organisational objectives.
- **Bargaining:** A more typical situation in which a conflict arises is due to fundamental differences in buying goals and objectives. This is usually true for new buying situations. In such a situation, conflict is resolved not by changing the differences in relative importance of the buying goals or objectives of the individuals involved, but by the process of bargaining. In this a single party is allowed to decide autonomously in the specific situation in return for some favouur or promise of reciprocity in future decisions.
- **Politicking:** When the earlier three fail, the parties may resort to tactics which may be unhealthy and lead to casting of aspersions on the dissenting members.

According to Sheth, both 'problem solving' and 'persuasion' are rational methods. Politicking and bargaining are considered as non-rational methods.

(4) The Individual Factors: In spite of the environmental, organisational, and interpersonal factors, it must be recognised that ultimately individuals, and not organisations, take buying decisions. Each member of the buying centre has a unique personality, a particular set of learned experience, a specified organisational function to perform, and perceptions of how best to achieve both personal and organisational goals. An industrial marketer should be aware of the differing buying perceptions and their influences on the ultimate buying decision. Perhaps, an understanding of the 'perceived risk and its management' at the individual level holds the key to identifying the individual influences on organisational buying behaviour in specific situations.

***The Perceived Risk*:** Newall defines decision-making as a risk taking activity and in this sense organisational buyer behaviour is seen as a risk handling behaviour. According to Newall, the factors, which affect the risk behaviour are:

Characteristics of the Purchase Problem: Some factors related to purchase problems are:

- size (rupee value) of the expenditure,

- degree of novelty contained in the type of buying task,
- degree of product essentiality,
- factors provoking purchase.

Characteristics of the Buyers: This includes:

- Buyer's level of general self-confidence.
- Buyer's level of specific self-confidence.
- Buyer's experience in playing the purchase role.
- Buyer's purchase history, i.e. of buying within a particular product area.
- Buyer's degree of technical and professional affiliations.

Organisational Environment: Some factors affecting the risks at the level of the company are:

- The size and financial standing of the organisational customer
- The degree of decision centralisation
- The degree of decision routinisation.

The Management of Perceived Risk: Basically, an individual visualises two types of risk:

- Performance risk—product may fail to come up to the performance standards
- Psychological risk—fear of being held responsible or accountable for the decision by other members

Both performance and psychological risk can be associated with the uncertainty concerning the outcome and the magnitude of the consequences associated with the wrong choice. Individual decision makers are motivated by a strong desire to reduce the level of risk in purchase decision. Research suggests the following categories of action to minimise the risk:

- external uncertainty reduction

  (e.g. visit supplier's plant)
- internal uncertainty reduction

  (e.g. consult with other buyers)
- external consequence reduction

  (e.g. multiple sourcing)
- internal consequences reduction

  (e.g. consult with company's top management)

Organisational buyers can also reduce the level of risk in purchasing situation by relying on familiar suppliers. This source loyalty provides a convenient method of risk minimisation. Similar to this, is a situation of placing orders on. 'high' credibility image suppliers in new buying situation.

An industrial marketer must make an attempt to understand and anticipate the areas of perceived risk and its minimisation by different members of the buying centre in specific buying situations. The knowledge may help them in developing effective selling strategies.

Q18. Describe the various buying situations.

Or

What were the characteristic featuresof:

(i) Straight Re-buy Situation

(ii) Modified Re-buy Situation

(iii) New Task Situation

Ans. An organisation needs to buy a variety of products and services to achieve its objectives. The 'buying basket' for a typical industrial customer may include products from any of the followink categories:

- Raw material — Steel, aluminium, iron ore,
- Major capital items — Blast Furnace, CNC machine tools,
- Minor Capital items — Industrial motors, pumps, valves,
- Fabricated components parts and sub-assemblies, and — Castings, sheet metal components, forgings
- Processed chemicals — Foundry chemicals, basic pharmaceutical formulations,
- Consumables — Lubricating oil, welding electrodes,
- Office equipment — Plain paper copiers, electronic typewriter,
- Services — Ttravel arrangement, transporters, housing, etc.

It should be easy for you to recognise that some products may be just one time purchases (major capital equipment), and others may be purchased frequently. The buying effort, in this sense, would be a function of the experience which the organisation may have for the different buying situations. Robinson, Faris and Wind have classified the various buying situations into three categories:

(1) Straight Re-buy Situation: This situation is similar to repeat buying situations of consumer/household buying. In this the buyer keeps on placing the order on routine basis without changing any product specifications (stationery items, chemicals, lubricants, abbrasives, paints are some examples). Some typical characteristics of the routine buying situations are:

- Routine purchasing procedures exist.
- The buying alternatives are known, but a formal or informal list of 'approved' suppliers is available.
- A supplier, not on list, is not considered.
- Decision on each separate transaction is made by the purchasing department.
- Buyers have relevant buying experience and require little new information.

(2) Modified Re-buy Situation: In a modified re-buy situation, a buyer may change the product specifications or may even change to a substitute product for economic and performance considerations. Thus,using aluminium instead of copper wires, nylon bushes instead of brass and using hydraulic excavators instead of mechanical are some examples. In this situation, some familiarity with either product or its performance expectations does exist. Some characteristics of the modified re-buy situations are:

- A regular requirement for the type of product exists.
- The buying alternatives are known, but sufficient change has occurred to require some alteration to the normal supply procedure.
- Change may be stimulated by external events, e.g. inputs from supplying companies.
- Change may be stimulated by internal events, e.g. new buying influences, value analysis, reorganisation.

(3) New Task Situation: 'New Task' is a situation where the organisational customer buys the product for the first time without having any previous experiences (personal computers, plain paper copiers, fax machines, CNC machine tools are some products for which little experience exist amongst a large number of the Indian organisation). Some of the characteristics, for 'new task' situations are:

- Need for the product has not arisen previously.
- Little or no past buying experience is available to assist in the purchasing decision.
- Members of the buying unit require a great deal of information.
- Alternative ways of meeting the need are likely to be under review.
- The situation occurs infrequently, but the decisions taken may set a pattern for more routine purchases subsequently.
- Opportunities exist at an early stage in the decision process for external (marketing) inputs to have an influence on the final decision made.

Q19. Explain the Fischer Model of organisational buying behaviour.

Ans. The central thesis of knowing and understanding the buyer behaviour is to anticipate the response of a buyer for different marketing stimuli surrounded by various environmental factors. Following is a simplified conceptual model highlighting this relationship.

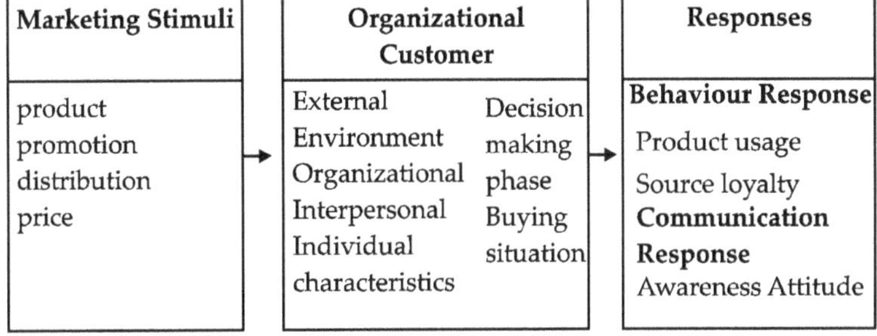

Fig. 1.4: A Simple Model of Organizational Behaviour

The conceptual model is indicative of the relationships and possible outcomes. However, a marketer's desire is to have a functional model with high degree of predictive reliability. In simple terms, he wants to have an answer as to "how" and "when" will he get the results. Desire to answer this question with high degree of consistency on predictive reliability has led to the development of a large number of models on organisational buying behaviour. It will be impossible to include each and every model.

The Fisher's Model: Following Figure illustrates this model:

Commercial Uncertainty	**Product Complexity**	
	Low	High
Low	Buyer emphasis (1)	Technologist emphasis (2)
High	Policy-maker emphasis (3)	Total involvement (4)

Low	**Product Complexity**	**High**
Standardized product	Differentiated product	
Technically simple	Technically complex	
Established product	New product	
Previously purchased	Initial purchase	
Existing application	New application Specialized	
Easy to install	installation	
No after-sales services	Technical after-sales service	

Factor in Product Complexity

Low	Commercial Uncertainty	High
Little investment	High investment	
Small order	Large order	
Short-term commitment	Long-term commitment	
No consequential adjustment	Substancial consequential adjustment	
Small potential effect on profitability	Large potential effect on profitability	
Easy to forecast effect	Hard to forecast effect	

Fig. 1.5: Fisher's Organizational Buying Behavior Model

As you would observe, the model attempts to identify the dominant influences along two main dimensions of any buying decision. These are product complexity and commercial uncertainty. The product complexity as well as the commercial uncertainties was low, .the purchase department (Buyer Emphasis Cell 1) played the dominant role in the buying decision. It was only after the short listing of the two, that the top management was involved. Fisher's conceptualization is an outstanding example of a simple representation of a very complex situation. In fact, it is a true representation of administrative arrangements and provisions which a large number of organizations have made to buy a vast heterogeneous array of products and services. The limitation, however, is absence of predictive ability.' It also fails to highlight the time dimension and the various steps in the buying decision exercise. Similar to the buy grid model, it facilitates in providing good insights of buying situations.

Q20. Discuss the criteria affecting the selection of suppliers by an organisation.

Ans. Here we will concentrate on the evaluation and selection criteria which organisations may adopt while selecting suppliers for the specific products or services. For instance, the purchase manager of an enterprise1 had received 15 quotations from different manufacturers of the desert coolers. He had then, based on a check list of attributes, short listed the two brands. Generally, these attributes cover product quality, reliability of the supplier, price and delivery. However, the attributes and their relative importance may vary for different product categories. Thus, in case of forgings, the importance ranking of vendor evaluation attributes by the automobile manufacturers was:

Ranking Order	Attribute
1	Reliability of delivery dates promised
2	Price
3	Supplier's flexibility
4	Consistency in dealings of the supplier
5	Rejection rates
6	Kind of manufacturing facilities
7	Efficient follow-up of the order
8	Persistent efforts to improve the quality of services
9	Prompt attention to enquiries
10	Suppliers overall reputation

Using the important attributes, members of the buying centre may then rate the suppliers against these attributes to identify the most attractive suppliers for forgings. After the ratings of the suppliers on these attributes, the members of the buying centre may like to negotiate with the preferred suppliers for better terms of prices and delivery schedules before making the final selection. Depending upon the situation, it may select one or many suppliers. Telco's price panels, to finalise the annual contracts for a large number of 'boughtouts', is a classic example of selecting vendors. Before inviting the suppliers for meeting with the 'price panel', Telco evaluates the suppliers on relevant attributes. After ensuring quality and reliability, it begins its negotiations on the commercial aspects covering price, delivery schedules and payment terms to arrive at mutually beneficial agreements for both the suppliers and Telco.

❑❑❑

2

Individual Influences on Buying Behaviour

Q1. What is meant by consumer perception? How do you justify the relevance of studying perception when they may not accurately reflect reality?

Ans. Perception is defined as the process by which an individual selects, organises, and interprets stimuli into a meaningful and coherent picture of the world. It can be described as "how we see the world around us." Two individuals may be exposed to the same stimuli under the same apparent conditions, but how each person recognises, selects, organizes, ad interprets these stimuli is a highly individual process based on each person's own needs, values, and expectations.

In order to appreciate the formation of perception, it is necessary to understand sensation. Sensation is the immediate response of our sensory receptors (e.g. eyes, ears, nose, mouth, fingers) to such basic stimuli as light, color, and sound. Perception, on the other hand, is the process by which these stimuli are selected, organised, and interpreted. Like a computer, we process raw data (sensation). However, the study of perception of focuses on what we add to or take away from these sensations as we assign meaning to them. That perception is subjective is illustrated by reaction to the Kamsutra Condoms and campaign. It was quite a controversial advertisement in India for the suggestive imagery and text for the message. However, some of us also saw the creative representation of what we had for traditions in India.

Relevance of Studying Perception: Human beings are constantly bombarded with stimuli during every minute and every hour of every day. The sensory world is made up of an almost infinite number of discrete sensations that are constantly and subtly changing. According to the principles of sensation, intensive stimulation "bounces off" most individuals, who subconsciously block a heavy bombardment of stimuli. Otherwise, the billions of different stimuli to which we are constantly exposed might serve to confuse us and keep us perpetually disoriented in a constantly changing environment. However, neither of these consequences tends to occur, because perception is not a function of sensory input alone. Rather, perception is the result of two different kinds of inputs that interact of form the personal pictures — the perceptions — that each individual experiences.

One type of input is 'physical stimuli' from the outside environment; the other type of input is provided by individuals themselves in the form of certain predispositions (expectations, motives, and learning) based on previous experience. The combination of these two very different kinds of inputs produces for each of us a very private, very personal picture of the world. Because each person is a unique individual, with unique experiences, needs, wants, desires, and expectations, it follows that each individuals perceptions are also unique. This explains why no two people see the world in precisely the same way.

Q2. Illustrate the stages of perception with a real or imaginary example.

Or

Describe the stages in perceptual process.

Ans. No consumer forms perception in a single step. Rather, perception is a outcome of a process consisting of the following parts:

- **Primitive Categorization:** Here, the basic characteristics of the stimulus are isolated by the person to form his perception. Thus, anything shining, may be seen with an amount of suspicious by the consumers. This is what is known as *primitive categorization.* A slight error of judgement on the part of the marketer in not appreciating this, may lead to a marketing pitfall. For instance, sample bottles of Sunlight, a dishwashing liquid in the US market, were mailed to consumers. The liquid contained 10 per cent lemon juice. Almost 80 people were treated at poison-centers after drinking some of the detergent. These individuals apparently assumed that the product was actually lemon juice, since many of the packaging cues resembled Minute Maid – a popular brand of frozen lemon juice.
- **Cue Check:** Here, the cue characteristics are analysed by the person in preparation for the selection of a schema. In the context of the sunlight liquid example quoted above, the cue check stage in the perceptual process was the pairing the yellow bottle with a prominent picture of a lemon.

- **Confirmation Check:** Here, once the schema is selected, a confirmation check is run by the person to see the validity of the schema chosen. In the context of the continuing example of the Sunlight liquid detergent, a juice schema was selected instead of a dishwashing liquid schema. The confirmatory check was the picture of the lemon juice as found on the leading brand of a reveal lemon juice.
- **Confirmation Completion:** The last and the final stage is confirmation completion where a perception is formed by the consumer or any person for that matter and decision is made. The act of drinking the detergent illustrates it. Unfortunately, the consumers found out their mistake the hardway.

Q3. What is meant by subliminal perception? What techniques are available in this regard?

Ans. People are also stimulated below their level of conscious awareness; that is, they can perceive stimuli without being consciously aware that they are doing so. Stimuli that are too weak or too brief to be consciously seen or heard may nevertheless by strong enough to be perceived by one or more receptor cells. This process is called *subliminal perception* because the stimulus is beneath the threshold, or 'limen," of conscious awareness, though obviously not beneath the absolute threshold of the receptors involved.

The effectiveness of so-called subliminal advertising was reportedly first tested at a drive-in movie in New Jersey in 1957, where the words "Eat popcorn" and "Drink Coca-Cola" were flashed on the screen during the movie. Exposure times were so short that viewers were unaware of seeing a message. It was reported that during the six-week test period, popcorn sales increased 58 per cent and Coca-Cola sales increased 18 per cent, but these findings were later reported to be false. Years later, a scientific study found that although the simple subliminal stimulus COKE served to arouse thirst in subjects, the subliminal command DRINK COKE did not have a greater effect, nor did it have any behavioural consequences.

Since the 1950s, there have been sporadic reports of marketers using subliminal messages in their efforts to influence consumption behaviour. For example, Disney was accused of using subliminal messages in the movie Aladdin (where the hero allegedly whispers "good teenagers, take off your clothes" in a subaudible voice), The Little Mermaid (where a minister officiating at a wedding ceremony allegedly displays an erection), and Lion King (where the letters "S-E-X" are allegedly formed in a cloud of dust). At times, it has been difficult to separate truth from fiction regarding such alleged manipulations. When some of the subliminal methods were tested methodically using scientific research procedures, the research results did not support the notion that subliminal messages can persuade consumers to act in a given manner.

Subliminal perceptions can be formed through several routes. The following are some techniques:

- **Embeds:** Embeds are tiny figures that are inserted into magazine advertising by use of high-speed photography or airbrushing. These hidden figures, usually of a sexual nature, supposedly exert strong but unconscious influences on innocent readers. Ice cubes are a prime culprit for accusations of this type of subliminal persuasion. Critics often focus on ambiguous shapes in drinks as evidence or the use of this technique. For instance, one ad of the Gilbey's Gin contains letter S E X are spelled out in the ice cubes.
- **Auditory Messages:** In addition to subliminal visual messages, many consumers and marketers seem to be fascinated by the possible effects of messages hidden on sound recordings. An attempt to capitalize on subliminal auditory perception techniques is found in the growing market for self-help cassettes. These tapes, which typically feature the sound of waves crashing or some other natural setting, supposedly contain subliminal messages to help that listener stop smoking, lose weight, gain confidence, and so on. Despite that rapid the rapid growth of this market, there is little evidence that subliminal stimuli transmitted on the auditory channel can bring about desired changes in behaviour.
- **Consumer Folklore:** Along with the interest in hidden self-help messages on recordings, some consumers have become concerned about marketing rumors, also called as the consumer folklore, of satanic messages recorded backward on rock records. The popular press has devoted much attention to such stories, and state legislatures have considered bills requiring warning labels about these messages. These backward messages do indeed appear on some albums, including Led Zeppelin's classic son "Stairway to Heaven" which contains the lyric "...there's still time to change." When played in reverse, this phrase sounds like "so here's to my sweet Satan." The novelty of such reversals might help to sell records, but the "evil" messages within have no effect. Humans do not have a speech perception mechanism operating at an unconscious level that is capable of decoding a reversed signal.
- **Low Level Auditory Stimulation:** One technique, known as 'psycho-acoustic persuasion', does appear to work. Subtle acoustical messages

such as "I am honest. I won't steal. Stealing is dishonest" are broadcast in more than 1000 stores in the United States to prevent shoplifting. Unlike subliminal perception, though, these messages are played at a (barely) audible level, using a technique known as *threshold messaging*. After a nine-month test period, theft losses in one six-store chain declined almost 40 per cent, saving the company $600,000.

To conclude, some evidence indicates, however, that these messages are affective only on individuals whose value systems make them predisposed to suggestion. For example, someone who might be thinking about taking something on a dare but who feels guilty about it might be susceptible to these messages, but they will not sway, a professional thief or a kleptomaniac.

Q4. How the sensory thresholds work?

Ans. Have you ever blown a dog whistle and watched pets respond to a sound you cannot hear? You are simply amazed by their power of sensation. The fact is that there are some stimuli that people simply are not capable of perceiving. And, of course, some people are better able to pick up sensory information than are others. The science that focuses on how the physical environment is integrated into our personal, subjective world is known as 'psychophysics'. By understanding some of the physical laws that govern what we are capable of responding to, this knowledge can be translated into marketing strategies. Thresholds work at the following levels.

- **The Absolute Threshold:** The absolute threshold refers to the minimum amount of stimulation that can be detected on a sensory channel. The sound emitted by a dog whistle is too high to be detected by human ears, so this stimulus is beyond our auditory absolute threshold. The absolute threshold is an important consideration in designing marketing stimuli. A billboard might have the most entertaining copy ever written, but this genius is wasted if the print is too small for passing motorists to see it from the highway.
- **The Differential Threshold:** The different threshold refers to the ability of a sensory system to detect changes or difference between two stimuli. A television commercial that is intentionally produced in black-and-white, might be noticed on a colour television because this decrease in the intensity of colour differs from the programme that preceded it. The same commercial being watched on a black-and-white television would not be seen as different and might be ignored altogether. A consumer's ability to detect a difference between two

stimuli is relative. A whispered conversation that might be unintelligible on a noisy street can suddenly become public and embarrassing knowledge in a quiet library. It is the relative difference between the decibel level of the conversation and its surroundings, rather than the loudness of the conversation itself, that determines whether the stimulus will register.

- **THE JND and Weber's Law:** The minimum change in a stimulus that can be detected is also known as the JND, which stands for Just Noticeable Difference. In the nineteenth century, a psychophysicist named Ernest Weber found that the amount of change that is necessary to be noticed is systematically related to the original intensity of the stimulus. The stronger the initial stimulus, the greater the change must be for it to be noticed. This relationship is known as Weber's Law. Many companies choose to update their packages periodically, making small changes that will not necessarily be noticed at the time.

Q5. Illustrate the sensory system.

Ans. External stimuli, or sensory inputs, can be received on a number of channels. We may see a billboard, hear a jingle, feel the softness of a cashmere sweater, taste a new flavour of ice cream, or smell a leather jacket. The inputs picked up by our five senses constitute the raw data that generates many types of responses. For example, sensory data emanating from the external environment (e.g. hearing a song on the radio) can generate internal sensory experiences when the song on the radio triggers a young man's memory of his childhood dance and brings to mind the soft feelings of the mothers touch. Sensory inputs evoke historic imagery, in which events that actually occurred are recalled. Fantasy imagery is the result when an entirely new, imaginary experience is the response to sensory data. These responses are an important part of hedonic consumption, or the multisensory, fantasy, and emotional aspects of consumers' interactions with products. the data that we receive from our sensory systems determine how we respond to products.

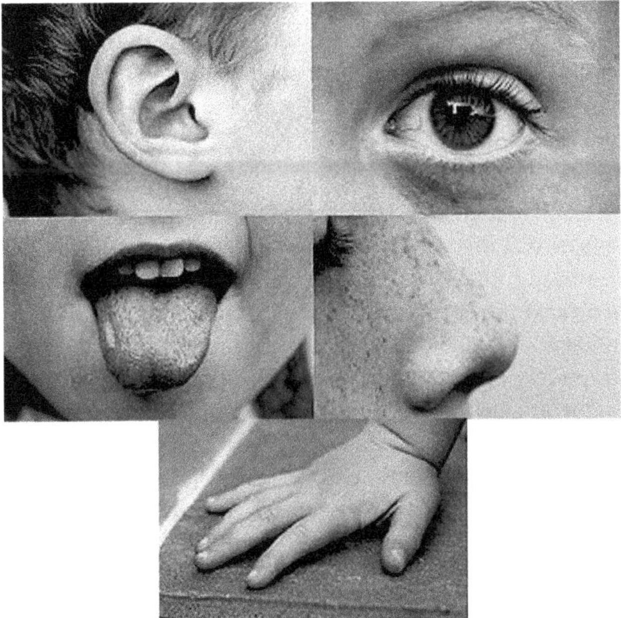

Fig. 2.1: Sensory System

- **Vision:** Marketers rely heavily on visual elements in advertising, store design, and packaging. Meanings are communicated on the visual channel through a product's size, styling, brightness, and distinctiveness from competitors. Colour is one of the most potent aspects of visual communication. Colours are rich in symbolic value and cultural meanings. For example, the display of green, white, and orange evokes feelings of patriotism for us. Such powerful cultural meanings make colour a central aspect of many marketing strategies.
- **Smell:** Odours can stir emotions or create a calming feeling. They can invoke memories or relieve stress. Some of our responses to scents result from early associations with other experiences. Consumers' love of fragrances has contributed to a very large industry. Indians spend well over 100 crores a year on perfume and have a very strong demand. No wonder that the Lakme and such multinationals as Revolon, have entered the market in a very big way.
- **Sound:** Music and sound are also important to marketers. Consumers buy millions of rupees worth of sound recordings each year, advertising jungles maintain brand awareness, and background music creates desired moods. The fight between the HMV, ZEE and the Plus Music

is well known now. Many aspects of sound may affect people's feelings and behaviours. Two areas of research that have widespread applications in consumer contexts are the effects of background music on mood and the influence of speaking rate on attitude change and message comprehension.

- **Touch:** Although relatively little research has been down on the effects of tactile stimulation on consumer behaviour, common observation tells us that this sensory channel is important. Moods are stimulated or relaxed on the basis of sensations of the skin, whether from a luxurious message or the bite of winter wind. The Lubriderm skin lotion ad shown the dramatically illustrates the use of tactile qualities to reinforce product attributes. Touch has even been shown to be a factor in sales interaction. In one study, for example, diners who were touched by wait people gave bigger tips, and food demonstrators in a supermarket who lightly touched customers had better luck in getting shoppers to try a new snack product and to redeem coupons for the brand.
- **Taste:** Our taste receptors obviously contribute to our experience of many products. Specialized companies called "flavor houses" keep busy trying to develop new tastes to please the changing palates of consumers. Their work has been especially important as consumers continue to demand good-tasting foods that are also low in calories and fat.

Q6. Explain the concept and typology of needs.

Ans. The concept of need and its typology has a long history and but the meaning is far from clear. Several terms like need, want and demand are used in the similar context. Thus, the particular form of consumption used to satisfy a need is termed a want. The specific way a need is satisfied depends upon the individual's unique history, learning experiences, and his or her cultural environment. For example, two coursemates in a training program, one Indian and the other French, may feel their stomachs rumbling during a lunchtime lecture. If neither person has eaten since the night before, the strength of their respective needs (hunger) would be about the same. However, the way each person goes about satisfying this need might be quite different. The first person may be aroused by prospect of a greasy *parantha* and *pakauris*, the second person may be a satisfied with cottage cheese, bread and milk. The distinction between needs and wants is important because it relates to the issue of whether marketers are actually capable of creating needs.

Types of Needs: People are born with a need for certain elements necessary to maintain life, such a food water, air and shelter. These are called *biogenic needs*. People have many other needs, however, that are not innate. *Psychogenic needs* are, acquired in the process of becoming a member of a culture. These include the need for status, power, affiliation, and so on. For example, that an Indian consumer may be driven to devote a good chunk of his income to products that permit him to display his concern for the family is an example of psychogenic needs. Consumers can also be motivated to satisfy either utilitarian or hedonic needs. The satisfaction of *utilitarian needs* implies that consumers will emphasize the objective, tangible attributes of products, such as durability in a home appliance fuel economy in a car etc. *Hedonic needs* are subjective and experiential. Consumers may rely on a product to meet their needs for excitement, self-confidence, fantasy, and so on. Of course, consumers may be motivated to purchase a product because it provides both types of benefits. For example, a Maruti car may be bought because it feels well styled, and luxurious and also because it keeps the cost of running the car low.

Q7. Illustrate the meaning of five level of the Maslow's hierarchy.

Ans. Maslow's hierarchy of needs is a theory in psychology, proposed by Abraham Maslow in his 1943 paper *A Theory of Human Motivation*. Maslow subsequently extended the idea to include his observations of humans' innate curiosity. His theories parallel many other theories of human developmental psychology, all of which focus on describing the stages of growth in humans. Maslow's hierarchy of needs is often portrayed in the shape of a pyramid, with the largest and most fundamental levels of needs at the bottom, and the need for self-actualization at the top.

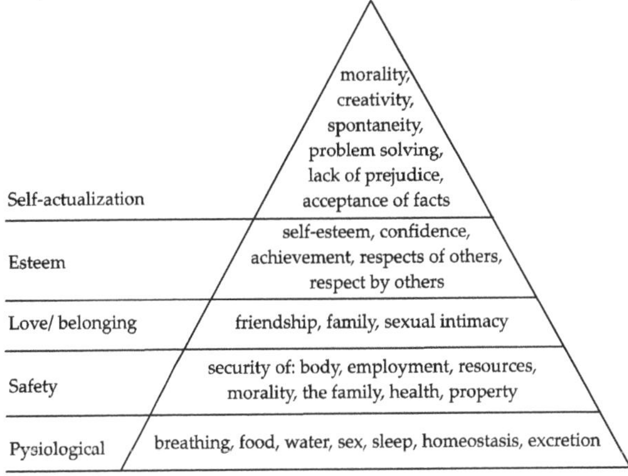

Fig. 2.2: Levels of Needs in the Maslow Hierarchy

Examples of product appeals tailored to each level are provided in Following Table.

Table 2.1: Maslow's Hierarchy and Marketing Strategies

Level of Hierarchy	Relevant Products	Example
Self-actualization Ego Needs	Hobbies, travel, education, cars, furniture, credit cards, stores, country clubs, liquors	Club Med: "The antidote for civilization" Royal Salute Scotch: "What the rich give the wealthy"
Belongingness	Clothing, grooming product, clubs, drinks	Pepsi: "You are in the Pepsi generation"
Safety	Insurance, alarm systems, retirement investments	Allstate Insurance: "You are in good hands with Allstate"
Physiological	Medicines, staple items, generics	Quaker Oat Bran "It's the right thing to do"

Q8. Describe motivation as a psychological force.

Ans. Motivation is the driving force within individuals that impels them action. This driving force is produced by a state of tension, which exists as the result of a reduce this tension through behaviour that they anticipate will fulfil their needs and thus relieve them of the stress they feel.

Needs: Every individual has needs: some are innate, others are acquired. Innate needs are physiological (i.e., biogenic); they include the needs for food, water, air, clothing, shelter, and sex. Because they are needed to sustain biological life, the biogenic needs are considered primary needs or motives.

Acquired needs are needs that we learn in response to our culture or environment. These may include needs for self-esteem, prestige, affection, power, and learning. Because acquired needs are generally psychological (i.e., psychogenic), they are considered secondary needs or motives. They result from the individual's subjective psychological state and from relationships with others. For example, all individuals need shelter from the elements; thus, finding a place to live fulfills an important primary need for a newly transferred executive. However, the kind of home she rents or buys may be the result of secondary needs. She may seek a place in which she and her husband can entertain large groups of people (and fulfill social needs): she may want to live in an exclusive community to impress her friends and family (and fulfill ego needs). The place where and individual ultimately chooses to live thus may serve to fulfill both primary and secondary needs.

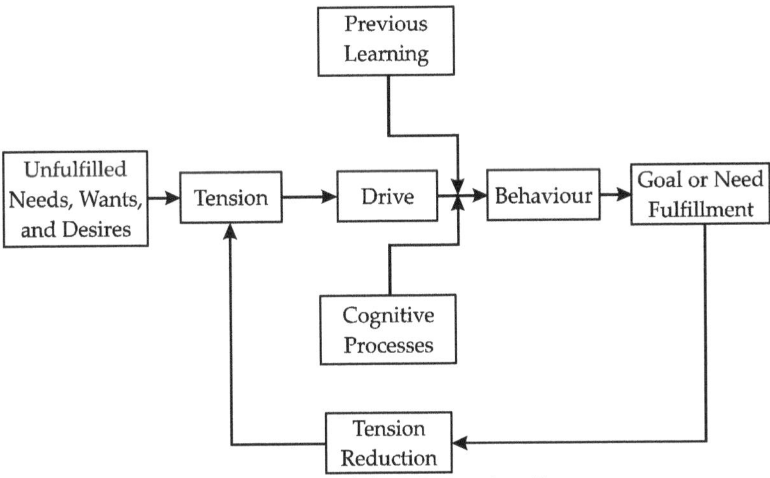

Fig. 2.3: Model of the Motivation Process

Goals: Individuals set goals on the basis of their personal values, and they select means (or behaviours) that they believe will help them achieve their desired goals. Figure A, B, and C depict a framework of the goal structure behind losing weight and maintaining weight loss and the results of a study based on this model. Figure A depicts an overall framework for pursuing consumption-related goals. Figure B depicts the inter-relationship among the needs driving the goal of losing weight (*e.g.*, increases self-confidence, looking and feeling better, and living longer) and the behaviours required to achieve the goal (*i.e.*, exercising and/or dieting). Figure C depicts the complex nature of goal setting based on subjects' responses to questions regarding their reasons for selecting weight loss as a goal, providing justification for each reason, and explaining each justification. The three diagrams together depict the complexity of goal setting and the difficulties in understanding this process through a set theoretical model. Figure depicts an ad that portrays subscribing to a health magazine as a means to achieve several physical appearance-related goals.

The selection of goals: An individual's personal characteristics and own perception of self also influence the specific goals selected. Research on personal goal orientation distinguished two types of people: (1) persons with promotion focus are interested in their growth and development, have more hopes and aspirations and favor are interested in safety and security, are more concerned with duties and obligations and favor the absence of negative out-comes. One study found, that in forming consumption-related goals, consumers with a prevention focus favored the status quo and inaction over action. Another study distinguished between two types of goals: (1) ideals, which represent hopes, wishes, and aspirations; and (2) oughts, which represent duties, obligations, and responsibilities. The study showed that people concerned with ideals relied more on feelings and affects in evaluating advertisements, while people more concerned with oughts relied more heavily on the substantive and factual contents of ads.

Positive and negative motivation: Motivation can be positive or negative in direction. We may feel a driving force toward some object or condition or a driving force away from some object or condition. For example, a person may be impelled toward a restaurant to fulfill a hunger need, and away from motorcycle transportation to fulfill a safety need.

Some psychologists refer to positive drives as needs, wants, or desires and to negative drives as fears or aversions. However, although positive and negative motivational forces seem to differ dramatically in terms of physical (and sometimes emotional) activity, they are basically similar in that both serve to initiate and sustain human behaviour.

Interdependence of needs and goals: Needs and goals are interdependent; neither exists without the other. However, people are often not as aware of their needs as they are of their goals. Individuals are usually somewhat more aware of their physiological needs than they are of their psychological needs. Most people know when they are hungry, thirsty, or cold, and they take appropriate steps to satisfy these needs. The same people may not consciously be aware of their needs for acceptance, self-esteem, or status. They may, however, subconsciously engage in behaviour that satisfies their psychological (acquired) needs.

Rational versus emotional motives: Some consumer behaviourists distinguish between so-called rational motives and emotional motives. They use the term rationality in the traditional economic sense, which assumes that consumers behave rationally by carefully considering all alternatives and choosing those that give them the greatest utility. In a marketing context, the term rationality implies that consumers select goals based on totally objective criteria, such as size, weight, price, or miles per gallon. Emotional motives imply the selection of goals according to personal or subjective criteria.

Q9.Write an essay on Theories of Motivation.

Ans. There are several principles on which the motivation theory is based. Some of them are explained below:

- **Instinct Theory of Motivation:** Early work on motivation described behaviour to instinct—the innate patterns of behaviour that are universal in species. This view is now largely discredited. For one thing, the existence of an instinct is difficult to prove or disprove. It is like saying that a consumer buys status symbols because he or she is motivated to attain status, which is hardly a satisfying explanation.

- **Drive Theory:** Drive theory focusses on biological needs that produce unpleasant states of arousal (e.g. your stomach grumbles during a morning class). We are motivated to reduce the tension caused by this arousal. Tension reduction has been proposed as a basic mechanism governing human behaviour. In marketing, tension refers to the unpleasant state that exists if a person's consumption needs are not fulfilled. A person may be grumpy if he hasn't eaten, or he may be dejected or angry if he cannot afford that new car he wants. This state activates goal-oriented behaviour, which attempts to reduce or eliminate this unpleasant state and return to a balanced one, is termed homeostasis. Drive theory, however, runs into difficulties when it tries to explain some facets of human behaviour that run counter to its predictions. People often do things that increase a drive state rather than decrease it. For example, people may delay gratification. If you know you are going out for a lavish dinner, you might decide to forego a snack earlier in the day even though you are hungry at that time. In other cases, people deliberately watch erotic movies, even though these stimuli often increase sexual arousal rather than diminish it.
- **Expectancy Theory:** Most current explanations of motivation focus on cognitive factors rather than biological ones to understand what drives behaviour. Expectancy theory suggests that behaviour is largely pulled by expectations of achieving desirable outcomes — positive incentives, rather than pushed from within. We choose one product over another because we expect this choice to have more positive consequences for us. Thus,the term drive is used here more loosely to refer to both physical and cognitive processes.

Q10. Argument for the development of an involvement profile.

Ans. A pair of French researchers have argued that no single component of involvement is predominant. Recognising that consumers can be involved with a product because it is a risky purchase and/or its use reflects upon or affects the self, they advocate the development of an involvement profile containing four components.

- Importance and risk (the perceived importance of the product and the consequences of bad purchase).
- Probability of making a bad purchase.

- Pleasure value of the product category.
- Sign value of the product category.

Q11. What do you understand by motivational conflicts?

Or

Write a short note on Motivational Conflicts.

Ans. A purchase decision may involve more than one source of motivation. Consumers often find themselves in situations where different motives, both positive and negative, conflict with one another, since marketers are attempting to satisfy consumers' needs, they can also be helpful by providing possible solutions to these dilemmas. Three general types of conflicts can occur: approach-approach, approach-avoidance, and avoidance-avoidance.

- **Approach-Approach:** Here, a person must choose between two desirable alternatives. A student might be torn between going home for the holidays and going on with friends for a sightseeing trip. Or, he or she might have to choose between two equally desired music albums but only one can be bought with the limited funds that they have.
- **Approach-Avoidance:** Many of the product and services we desire have negative consequences attached to them as well. We may feel guilty or ostentatious when buying ice creams or expensive perfume. Some solutions to these conflicts include the proliferation of fake furs, which eliminate guilt about harming animals to make a fashion statement, and the success of diet foods, such as Weight Watchers, that promise good food without the calories. Many marketers try to overcome guilt by convincing consumers that they are deserving of luxuries. The conflict of this kind gives rise to another consumer behavior concept, called cognitive dissonance. The theory of cognitive dissonance is based on the premise that people have a need for order and consistency in their lives and that a state of tension is created when beliefs or behaviors conflict with one another. A state of dissonance occurs when there is a logical inconsistency between two or more beliefs or behaviors. It often occurs when a consumer must make a choice between two products, where both alternatives usually possess both good and bad qualities. By choosing one product and not the other, the person gets the bad qualities of the chosen product and loses out on the good qualities of the unchosen one. This loss creates an unpleasant, dissonant state that the person is motivated to

reduce. The conflict that arises when choosing between two alternatives may be resolved through a process of cognitive dissonance reduction, in which people are motivated to reduce this inconsistency (or dissonance) and thus, eliminate unpleasant tension. People tend to convince themselves after the fact that the choice they made was the smart one by finding additional reasons to support the alternative they chose, or perhaps by "discovering" flaws with the option they did not choose. A marketer can resolve an approach-avoidance conflict by bundling several benefits together.

- **Avoidance-Avoidance:** Sometimes consumers find themselves caught "between a rock and hard place." They may face a choice with two undesirable alternatives. A person may be faced with the option of either throwing more money into an old car or buying a new car. Marketers frequently address this conflict by message that stress the unforeseen benefits of choosing one option (e.g., by emphasizing lease finance or easy payment plans to ease the pain of new-car payments). Similarly, the problem of remaining unemployed or taking up a job which is either life threatening or socially low. Medicine buying is another example of this type of conflict.

Q12. Define the term of consumer involvement.

Ans. Along with the concept of motivation, involvement is another concept which central to activating consumer motives. Involvement refers to "the level of perceived personal importance and/or interest evoked by a stimulus (or stimuli) within a specific situation".

This definition implies that aspects of the person, the product, and the situation all combine to determine the consumer's motivation to process product related information at a given point in time. When consumers are intent on doing what they can to satisfy a need, they will be motivated to pay attention and process any information felt to be relevant to achieving their goals. On the other hand, a person may not bother to pay any attention to the same information it is not seen as relevant to satisfying some need. One person who prides himself on his knowledge of exercise equipment may read anything he can find about the subject, spend his spare time in athletics stores, and so on, while another (lazier) person may skip over this information without giving it a second thought.

Involvement can be viewed as the motivation to process information. To the degree that there is a perceived linkage between a consumer's needs, goals, or values, and product knowledge, the consumer will be motivated to pay attention to product information. When relevant knowledge is activated in memory, a motivational state is created that drives behaviour (e.g. shopping). This subjective feeling of personal relevance is termed felt involvement. As felt involvement with a product increases, people devote more attention to ads related to the product, exert more cognitive effort to understand these ads, and focus their attention on the product-related information in them.

Degree of involvement can be conceived as a continuum, ranging from absolute lack of interest in a marketing stimulus at one end to obsession at the other. Consumption of the low end of involvement is characterised by inertia, where decisions are made out of habit because the consumer lacks the motivation to consider alternatives. At the high end of involvement, we can expect to find the type of passionate intensity reserved for people and objects that carry great meaning to the individual.

Involvement also affects the information processing and activation. Thus, type of information processing depends upon the consumem's level of involvement. It can range from simple processing, where only the basic features of a message are considered to the one all the way to elabouuuration, where the incoming information is linked to one's pre-existing knowledge systems.

Q13. Explain the facets of involvement.

Ans. Involvement can take many forms. A consumer could certainly be said to be involved with a pair of running shoes if they help to define and bolster his self-concept. This involvement seems to increase at certain times, as when he must prove himself in a competition. Alternatively, the act of buying the shoes may be very involving for people who are passionately devoted to shopping.

Types of Involvement: It seems that involvement is a fuzzy concept, because it overlaps with other things and means different things to different people. Indeed, the consensus is that there are actually several broad types of involvement.

- **Purchase Involvement:** Purchase involvement is related to a consumer's level of interest in the buying process that is triggered by the need to consider a particular purchase. Many sales promotions are designed to increase purchase involvement. For instance, in a contest sponsored by a perfume company, women submitted details of their most intimate trysts by letter or by phone to radio talk shows. The winning stories were edited into a romance novel published by the manufacturer. These books, in turn, were given away as a gift with the purchase of the perfume. Sales was reported to have shot up as a result.
- **Message-Response Involvement:** Message-response involvement

refers to the processing of marketing communication. Television is considered a low involvement medium, because it requires a passive viewer who exerts relatively little control (remote control "zipping" notwithstanding) over content. In contrast, print is high-involvement medium. The reader is actively involved in processing the information and is able to pause and reflect on what he or she has read before moving on.

- **Ego Involvement:** Ego involvement, sometimes termed enduring involvement, refers to the importance of a product to a consumer's self-concept. For example, the consumer's running shoes are clearly an important part of his self-identity (*i.e.,* they are said to have high sign value). This type of involvement is independent of particular purchase situations.

Q14. What is meant by multi-attribute attitude modes?

Or

Explain the Multi Attributes Attitude Models with suitable examples.

Or

Define the following models:

(i) ATO Model.

(ii) BI Model.

Or

Write a short note on Multi attribute Attitude Model.

Ans. Consumers are individuals with likes and dislikes. When the preponderance of people in a particular group feel one way or another about a product, service, entity, person, place or thing, it is said to be a generalized consumer attitude that could affect the marketing of that person, product or entity in positive or negative ways. Marketers strive to influence consumer attitudes, and understanding the prevailing attitude is the first step to changing it if needed. Model-making in attitudes have been attempted in a variety of ways. Most prominent among them are the multi-attribute attitude models. Given below is an account of the same.

Multi-attribute attitude models explain how consumers may combine their beliefs about product attributes to form their attitudes about various brand alternatives. These models assume that the brand which receives the best attitude, will be chosen. They further assume that consumers will go through the standard Hierarchy of Effects sequence (i.e. Awareness – Interest – Desire – Action).

A careful scrutiny of all multi-attribute attitude models establishes two general categories of these models. Category I comprises the models that Emphasise the Attitude—Toward—Objects. Hence, they are termed as ATO models. Category II consists of those models that focus on predicting the behavioural intentions (BI) of consumers to perform certain action.

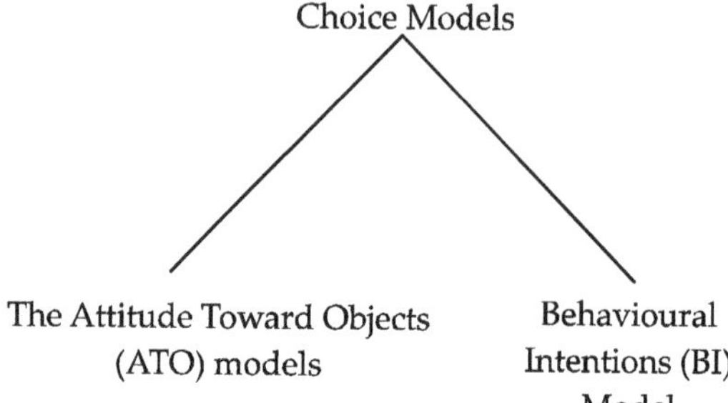

Fig. 2.4: Multi-altributes of Choice Models

The Attitude—Toward—Objects (ATO) Models: Although a variety of ATO models are found in consumer research; most of these models seek information on the importance of brand attributes; beliefs about the presence or absence of those attributes in the brand alternatives and information on their combined effect in alternative evaluation. Fishbein's model (1972) represents this genre of models. Algebraically, the model is expressed as:

$$A_0 = \sum_{i=1}^{n} B_i a_i$$

where,

A_0 = the overall attitude toward object 'O'

B_i = the belief of whether or not object 'O' has a particular attribute

a_i = the importance rating of the attributes

n = the number of beliefs

(2) The Behavior Intentions (BI) Model: The BI model is in effect, an extension of Fishbein's ATO model. The model does not attempt to predict behavior *per se* but intentions to behave algebraically, the model are as follows:

$$B \approx BI = W_1 (A_B) + W_2 (SN)$$

Where,

B = Behavior

BI = Behavior Intention

A_B = attitude towards performing the behavior

SN = the subjective norm

W_1 and W_2, are empirically determined weights, through regression analysis.

A_B and SN are obtained directly from consumers via questionnaires. Thus, A_B is obtained from the following equation:

where,

$$A_B = \sum_{i=1}^{n} b_i e_i$$

A_B = attitude towards the behaviour

b_i = the person's belief that performing the behaviour will result in onsequence

e_i = the person's evaluation of consequence

n = the number of beliefs

The above equation has one major difference over the earlier Fishbein's ATO Model. It is that the BI Model assesses the person's belief that performing a particular behavior will result in a particular consequence. They are termed as Subjective Norms (SN). The equation for obtaining the subjective norms is as follows:

$$SN = \sum_{j=1}^{n} NB_j \; MC_j$$

where,

SN = subjective norm

NB_j = the normative belief that a reference group of persons j thinks that the consumer should or should not perform the behavior

MC = the motivation to comply with the influence of the referent j and

n = number of relevant reference groups of individuals.

Various research studies have found the BI model to be superior to the standard multi-attribute choice models, though eye-brows have been raised concerning the calculation of the subjective norms (SN). In practice, this exercise is never so simple.

Q15. Among the attitude-change strategies describe the Functional Approach.

Ans. Altering consumer attitudes is a key strategy consideration for most marketers. For marketers who are fortunate enough to be market leaders and to enjoy a significant amount of customer goodwill and loyalty, the overriding goal is to fortify. The existing positive attitudes of customers so that they will not succumb to competitors' special offers and other inducements designed to win them over.

An effective strategy for changing consumer attitudes towards a product or brand is to make particular needs prominent. One method for changing motivation is known as the *functional approach*. According to this approach, attitudes can be classified in terms of four functions: the utilitarian function, the ego-defensive function, the value-expressive function, and the knowledge function.

- **The Utilitarian Function:** We hold certain brand attitudes partly because of a brand's utility. When a product has been useful or helped us in the past, our attitude towards it tends to be favourable. One way of changing attitudes in favouur of a product is by showing people that it can serve a utilitarian purpose that they may not have considered. For example, the ad for Lysol point out that this product kills harmful germs.
- **The Ego-defensive Function:** Most people want to protect their self – images from inner feelings of doubt — they want to replace their uncertainty with a sense of security and personal confidence. Ads for cosmetics and fashion clothing, by acknowledging this need, increase both their relevance to the consumer and the likelihood of a favouurable attitude change by offering reassurance to the consumer's self-concept. For example, a retailer of fashion clothing, stresses in its headline: "When I believe in myself, everything becomes possible."
- **The Value-expressive Function:** Attitudes are an expression or reflection of the consumer's general values, lifestyle, and outlook. If a consumer segment generally holds a positive attitude towards owning the latest designer jeans, then their attitudes towards new brands of designer jeans are likely to reflect that orientation. Similarly, if a segment of consumers has a positive attitude towards being "high tech," then their attitudes towards thin wall-mountable HDTV set are likely to reflect this viewpoint. Thus, by knowing target consumers' attitudes, marketers can better anticipate their values, lifestyle, or outlook and can reflect these characteristics in their advertising and direct-marketing efforts.
- **The Knowledge Function:** Individuals generally have a strong need to know and understand the people and things they encounter. The consumer's "need to know," a cognitive need, is important to marketers concerned with product positioning. Indeed, many product and brand positioning are attempts to satisfy the *need to know* and to improve the consumer's attitudes towards the brand by emphasizing its advantages over competitive brands. For instance, a message for a

new OTC allergy medication might point out how it is superior to other OTC allergy medications in alleviating the symptoms of allergies. The message might even use a bar graph to contrast its allergy symptom relief abilities to other leading allergy medications.

Q16. What is the relationship between attitude and consumer decision-making?

Ans. In everyday life, consumers receive a variety of marketing communications about what they should buy and they should not. They come to know about different claims and standings of the brands. On the basis of inputs received from various sources, consumers develop their assessment of the brands, better known as the *brand-image*. The brand image helps consumers in believing which brand is more likely to have a particular benefit or a feature (technically known as the *product attribute*). It should be noted here that since these brand beliefs are based on consumer perception, they may sometimes be at variance with reality. Thus, a potential car buyer may believe that the brand A of car has style but it may not be actually true about the brand A. In a similar vein, a potential lipstick buyer may believe that the brand B of the lipstick has the attribute of social prestige. In reality, it may not be so.

Thus, consumer attitude are based on the perception, true or otherwise. But they provide a very important clue as to whether the consumers will take a particular course of action or not. Thus, a person after having been bombarded by a string of newspapers ads on various TV brands available in India, may suddenly observe: "Oh, the TV ads! I can't stand them any more!" Similarly, a typical housewife may have this to say to her husband, after having viewed the sunday morning transmission: "You know something, the TV ads are so fascinating that they have taught a lot to our children in making brand choices for grocery".

These two statements express a summary evaluation of a marketing stimulus, i.e. promotional methods, and indicate how these will act in case of consumers who were asked to respond. Thus, the first consumer will probable zap the TV commercials or skip them. The second housewife may regulate the viewing hours of the television for the children.

Q17. Define learning. What are the theories of learning?

Or

Write a short note on Theories of Learning.

Or

Write a short note on Cognitive Theory of Learning.

Or

Differentiate between classical and operant conditioning.

Or

Write a short note on Instrumental Conditioning.

Or

Clearly distinguish between classical and instrumental conditioning as theories of consumer learning.

Ans. Learning refers to a relatively permanent change in behavior that is caused by experience. A more detailed definition of learning is when it is viewed "as a process in which behavioral capabilities are changed as result of experience provided the change can not be accounted for by native response tendencies, maturation or any temporary states of the organism due to fatigue, drugs, or any other temporary factors". The key words of the definition are: process; behavioral capabilities; and an enduring change. Thus, learning is not an act; it is not the behavior but the capability to behave and the permanency of the change through the experience. This experience does not have to acquire directly by the learner. He can learn vicariously too – by observing events that affect others. He also learns even when he is not trying. Consumers recognize many brand names and can hum many product jingles, for example, even for those product categories they themselves do not use. This casual, unintentional acquisition of knowledge is known as incidental learning. Like the concepts of perception and motivation discussed in the last two units, learning is a process. Our knowledge about the world is constantly being revised as we are exposed to new stimuli and receive ongoing feedback that allows us to modify behavior in other similar situations.

Theories of Learning

- **Classical Conditioning:** Classical conditioning occurs when a stimulus that elicits a response, is paired with another stimulus that initially does not elicit a response on its own. Over time, this second stimulus causes a similar response because it is associated with the first stimulus. This phenomenon was first demonstrated in dogs by Ivan Pavlov, a Russian physiologists doing research on digestion in animals. Pavlov conducted a number of conditioning trials by pairing a neutral stimulus (a bell) with a stimulus known to cause a salivation response in dogs (he squirted dried meat powder into their mouths). The powder was an Unconditioned Stimulus (UCS) because it was naturally capable of causing the response. Overtime, the bell became a Conditioned Stimulus (CS). it did not initially cause salivation, but the dogs learned to associate the bell with the meat powder and began to salivate at the sound of the bell only The drooling of these canine consumers over a sound, now linked to feeding time, was a

Conditioned Response (CR). Classical conditioning can have similar effects for more complex reactions, too. Even a credit card becomes a conditioned cue that triggers greater spending, especially since it is a stimulus that is present only in situations where consumers are spending money. People learn they can make larger purchases when using credit cards, and they also have been found to leave larger tips than when using cash. Small wonder that American Express reminds us, "don't leave home without it."

- **Operant Conditioning:** Operant conditioning, also known as instrumental conditioning, occurs as the individual learns to perform behaviors that produce positive outcomes and to avoid those that yield negative outcomes. This learning process is most closely associated with the psychologist B.F. Skinner, who demonstrated the effects of instrumental conditioning by teaching animals to dance, play ping-pong, and so on by systematically rewarding them for desired behaviors. While responses in classical conditioning are involuntary and fairly simple, those in instrumental conditioning are made deliberately to obtain a goal and may be more complex. The desired behavior may be learned over a period of time, as intermediate actions are rewarded in a process called shaping. For example, the owner of a new store may award prizes to shoppers just for coming in, hoping that over time they will continue to drop in and eventually buy something. A good way to remember the difference is to keep in mind that in instrumental learning, the response is performed because it is instrumental to gaining a reward or avoiding a punishment. Consumers over time come to associate with people that reward them and to choose products that make them feel good or satisfy some need. Instrumental learning occurs in one of the following ways. When the environment provides *positive reinforcement* in the form of a reward, the response is strengthened and appropriate behavior is learned. For example, a woman who gets compliments after wearing Lakme perfume will learn that using this product has the desired effect, and she will be more likely to keep buying the product. *Negative reinforcement* also strengthens responses so that appropriate behavior is learned. A foot-wear manufacturer recently ran an ad showing a woman in embarrassment as her slipper broke off in the middle of the market. The message is that she could have avoided this negative outcome if only she had used the manufactures brand of footwear.
- **Cognitive Learning Theory:** Cognitive learning explains learning as a result of mental processes. In contrast to behavioral theories of

learning, cognitive learning theory stresses the importance of internal mental processes. This perspective views people as problem solvers who actively use information from the world around them to master their environment. Supporters of this viewpoint also stress the role of creativity and insight during the learning process. The cognitive theory explanations of learning are strongly based on memory, memory processes.

Q18. What are the issues of learning?

Ans. The Issue of Consciousness: A lot of controversy surrounds the issue of whether or when people are aware of their learning processes. While behavioural learning theorists Emphasise the routine, automatic nature of conditioning, proponents of cognitive learning argue that even these simple effects are based on cognitive factors. On the other hand, there is some evidence for the existence of non-conscious procedural knowledge. People apparently do process at least some information in an automatic, passive way, which is a condition that has been termed mindlessness. When we meet someone new or encounter a new product, for example, we have a tendency to respond to the stimulus in terms of existing categories, rather than taking the trouble to formulate different ones. Our reactions are activated by a trigger feature, some stimulus that cues us towards a particular pattern. For example, the presence of a doctor in a message about the tooth paste, prompted the consumers to rate the product superior although none of them ever consulted a dentist before they bought their tooth paste. Nonetheless, many modem theorists are beginning to regard some instances of conditioning as cognitive processes, especially where expectations are formed about the linkages between stimuli and responses. Indeed, studies using masking effects, where it is difficult for subjects to learn CS/UCS associations; show substantial reductions in conditioning. For example, an adolescent girl may observe that women on television and in real life seem to be rewarded with compliments and attention when they smell nice and wear alluring clothing. She figures out that the probability of these rewards occurring is greater when she wears perfume, and deliberately wears a popular scent to obtain the payoff of social acceptance.

Observational Learning: Observational learning occurs when people watch the actions of others and note the reinforcements they receive for their behaviours. This type of learning is a complex process. People store these observations in memory as they accumulate knowledge, perhaps using this information at a later point to guide their own behaviour. This process of imitating the behaviour of others is called *modeling*. For example, a woman shopping for a new kind of perfume may remember the reaction her friend received upon wearing a certain brand several months earlier, and she will base her, behaviour on her friend's actions.

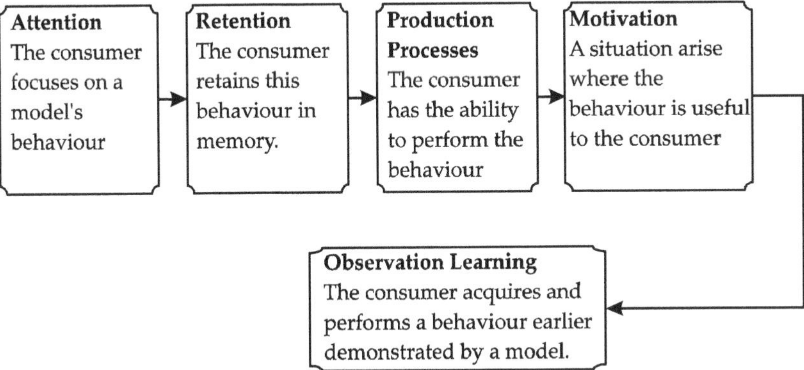

Fig. 2.5: Components of Observational Learning

In order for observational learning in the form of modeling to occur, four conditions must be met:

- The consumer's attention must be directed to the appropriate model, who for reasons of attractiveness, competence, status, or similarity is desirable to emulate.
- The consumer must remember what is said or done by the model.
- The consumer must convert this information into actions.
- The consumer must be motivated to perform these actions.

Q19. Elabouuurate the structure and functioning of memory.

Or

Should marketer work at the short-term memory or the long-term memory? How are the two related?

Ans. Memory involves a process of acquiring information and storing it over time so that it will be available when needed. Contemporary approaches to the study of memory employ an information-processing approach. They assume that the mind is in some ways like a computer, data are input, processed, and output for later use in revised form. In the encoding stage, information is entered in a way the system will recognise. In the storage stage, this knowledge is integrated with what is already in memory and "warehoused" until needed. During retrieval, the person accesses the desired information.

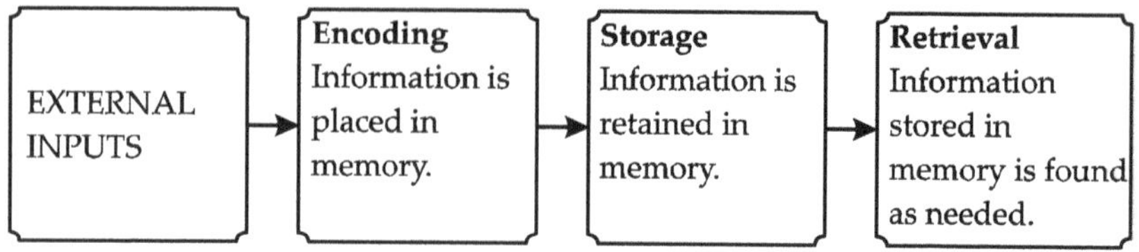

Fig. 2.6: The Memory Process

According to the information-processing approach, there are three distinct memory systems: sensory memory, short-term memory (STM), and long-term memory (LTM).

- **The sensory memory** permits storage of the information we receive from our senses. This storage is very temporary; it lasts a couple of seconds at most. For example, a person might be walking past a pastry shop and get a quick, enticing whiff of something baking inside. While this sensation would only last for a few seconds, it would be sufficient to allow the person to determine if he or she should investigate further. If the information is retained for further processing, it passes through an attentional gate and is transferred to short-term memory.
- **Short-term memory** also stores information for a limited period of time and its capacity is limited. Similar to a computer, this system can be regarded as working memory; it holds the information we are currently processing. Verbal input may be stored acoustically (in terms of how it sounds) or semantically (in terms of its meaning). The information is stored by combining small pieces into larger ones in a process known as "chunking." A chunk is a configuration that is familiar to the person and can be manipulated as a unit. For example, a brand name can be a chunk that summarizes a great deal of detailed information about the brand. Initially, it was believed that short-term memory is capable of processing between five to nine chunks of information at a time, and for this reason phone numbers were designed to have seven digits. It now appears that three to four chunks is the optimum size for efficient retrieval (seven-digit phone numbers can be remembered because the individual digits are chunked, so we may remember a three-digit exchange as one piece of information). Initially it was believed that short-term memory is capable of processing between five to nine chunks of information at a time, and for this reason phone numbers were designed to have seven digits. It now appears that three to four chunks is the optimum size for efficient retrieval (seven-digit phone numbers can be remembered because the individual digits are chunked, so we may remember a thrcc-digit

exchange as one piece of information).

- **Long-term memory** is the system that allows us to retain information for a long period of time. In order for information to enter into long-term memory from short-term memory, elabouuurate rehearsal is required. This process involves thinking about the meaning of a stimulus and relating it to other information already in memory. Marketers sometimes assist in the process by devising catchy slogans or jingles that consumers repeat on their own.

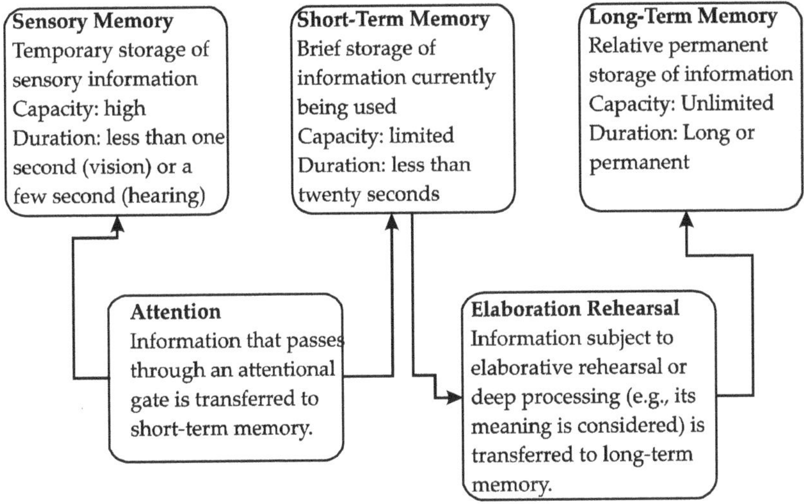

Fig. 2.7: Relationships among Memory Systems

Q20. Mention most important characteristics of the jeans market in India.

Ans. At a time when there are a number of players in the Rs. 2,000 crore Jeans market in India, the manufacturers, both foreign and Indian are using personality and the associations formed with image, legend and symbolism, rather than style, quality or material, for their brands. The principle behind the process of forging unique personalities for brands is that consumers of a particular brand of jeans consider themselves part of a tribal brotherhood.

Some of the personality building measures adopted by players in the Indian market are as follows:

- Levi Strauss, the fully owned subsidiary of the $5.6 billion Levi Strauss & Co. is linking its target customer to legendary rebels like Marlon Brando and James Dean simultaneously stressing the image of individuality that the brand confers on its wearer. The message is that Levi's is for mavericks and loners who identify with challengers to orthodoxy.

- Lee Jeans which are being marketed by Arvind Fashions—a joint venture between the Rs. 450 crore Arvind Mills and the $4.5 billion VF corp. of the US—is single-mindedly conjuring up the image of the young American whom everybody admires. The intention is to establish its heritage and the American character of the brand.
- Pepe, the subsidiary of the UK based 250 million pounds Pepe Jeans is communicating the persona of the urban, sophisticated European as opposed to the all American hunk, to appeal to a different breed of buyers. They are trying to create a classy, chic and trendy personality in the European way.
- Lee Cooper, niarxeted in the country by its licensee, the Rs. 3 crore Indus Clothing, is using its campaign to paint a portrait of a young, foreign male, at home somewhere in a European city. The idea is to convey a feeling of being a person who is in sync with the aspirations of the go getters.
- Dupont Sportswear, which markets Wrangler jeans, is targeting the young college goer who dreams of heroic exploits by combining visuals of the Wild West and cowboys, with slogans relating to campus life and in turn contemporarising the cowboy image.
- For its Flying Machine jeans, Arvind Mills uses the image as a happy go lucky student, intent on getting the most out of life. The image is being projected to weave an aura of confidence and assurance without aggression.

Q21. What is personality? Describe the theories that have been proposed on personality.

Or

Explain the Trait Theory of Personality with suitable examples.

Or

Write a short note on Trait Theory of Personality.

Or

Write a short note on Theories of Personality.

Or

Does the self concept theory explain the influence of self concept on consumption?

Ans. The study of personality has been approached by theorists in a variety of ways. Some have Emphasised the dual influence of heredity and early childhood experiences on personality development; others have stressed broader social and environmental influences and the fact that personalities develop continuously over time. Some theorists prefer to view personality as a unified whole; others focus on specific traits. The wide variation in viewpoints makes it difficult to arrive at a single definition. However, we propose that personality can be defined as "those inner psychological characteristics that both determine and reflect how a person responds to his or her environment."

The emphasis in this definitions is on inner characteristics – those specific qualities, attributes, traits, factors, and mannerisms that distinguish one individual from other individuals. The deeply ingrained characteristics that we call personality are likely to influence the individual's product choices: They affect the way consumers respond to marketers' promotional efforts, and when, where, and how they consumer particular products or services. Therefore, the identification of specific personality characteristics associated with consumer behaviour has proven to be highly useful in the development of a firm's market segmentation strategies.

Theories of Personality: There are several theories that have been proposed on personality. While there is no agreement on exactly how personality influences behaviour, there are at least four distinct approaches that are known to have implications for developing the marketing mix and for segmentation. Each of these theories has played a prominent role in studying the relationship between consumer personalities and their behaviour.

(1) Freudian Theory: Sigmund Freud's *psychoanalytic theory of personality* is a cornerstone of modern psychology. This theory was built on the premise that unconscious needs or drives, especially sexual and other biological drives, are at the heart of human motivation and personality. Freud constructed his theory on the basis of patients' recollections of early childhood experiences, analysis of their dreams, and the specific nature of their mental and physical adjustment problems.

(2) Trait theory: Trait theory constitutes a major departure from the qualitative measures that typify the Freudian and neo-Freudian movements (e.g. personal observation, self-reported experiences, dream analysis, projective techniques).

The orientation of trait theory is primarily quantitative or empirical; it focuses on the measurement of personality in terms of specific psychological characteristics, called *traits*. A trait is defined as "any distinguishing, relatively enduring way in which one individual differs from another. Trait theorists are concerned with the construction of personality tests (or inventories) that enable them to pinpoint individual differences in terms of specific traits.

Selected single – trait personality tests (which measure just one trait, such as self-confidence) are often developed specifically for use in consumer behaviour studies. These tailor-make personality tests measure such traits as consumer innovativeness (how receptive a person is to new experiences), consumer materialism (the degree of the consumer's attachment to "worldly possessions"), and consumer ethnocentrism (the consumer's likelihood to accept or reject foreign-made products).

(3) Neo-Freudian personality Theory: Several of Freud's colleagues disagreed with his contention that personality is primarily instinctual and sexual in nature. Instead, these neo-Freudians believed that *social relationship* are fundamental to the formation and development of personality. For instance, Alfred Adler viewed human being as seeking to attain various rational goals, which he called *style of life.* He also placed much emphasis on the individual's efforts to overcome *feeling of inferiority* (i.e., by striving for superiority).

Harry Stack Sullivan, another neo-Freudian, stressed that people continuously attempt to establish significant and rewarding relationships with others. He was particularly concerned with the individual's efforts to reduce tensions, such as anxiety.

Like Sullivan, Karen Horney was also interested in *anxiety.* She focused on the impact of child-parent relationships and the individual's desire to conquer feelings of anxiety. Horney proposed that individuals be classified into three personality groups: *compliant, aggressive,* and *detached.*

- Compliant individuals are those who move towards others (they desire to be loved, wanted, and appreciated).
- Aggressive individuals are those who move against others (they desire to excel and win admiration).
- Detached individuals are those who move away from others (they desire independence, self-reliance, self-reliance, self-sufficiency, and individualism or freedom from obligations).

(4) Self Concept Theory: This theory holds that individuals have a concept of self based on who they think they are (the actual self) and a concept of who they think they would like to be (the ideal self). Self concept theory is related to psychoanalytic theory since the actual self is similar to the ego and the ideal self is similar to the superego. Self concept theory is governed by the desire to attain self consistency and the desire to enhance one's self esteem. Generally, consumers buy products that confirm to their actual self image. But if they are low in self esteem they are more likely to buy based on what they would like to be rather than what they are.

Buying to achieve an unrealizable self image can lead to compulsive purchasing behavior. Frequent purchasing is a means to overcome the discrepancy between the real and ideal selves and to relieve a sense of low self esteem. Another dimension of self concept theory is the extended self. Certain products have symbolic value and are considered an extension of our personality (e.g. a car). This extension of self concept theory in fact has been called symbolic interactionism because it emphasizes the interaction between individuals and the symbols in their environment. Advertisers have understood the symbolic role of products in influencing self image. Advertising for jewellery, cosmetics, automobiles and clothing frequently communicates an image of the user. Compared to other attitudes, the self-concept is a very complex structure. It is composed of many attributes, some of which are given greater emphasis in determining overall self-attitude. Attributes of self-concept can be described along such dimensions as their content (e.g., facial attractiveness versus mental aptitude), positivity or negativity (i.e., self-esteem), intensity, stability over time, and accuracy (i.e., the degree to which one's self-assessment corresponds to reality). As will be seen later in the unit, consumers' self-assessments can be quite distorted, especially with regard to their physical appearance.

Buying to achieve an unrealisable self image can lead to compulsive purchasing behaviour. Frequent purchasing is a means to overcome the descrepancy between the real and ideal selves and to relieve a sense of low self esteem.

Another dimension of self concept theory is the extended self. Certain products have symbolic value and are considered an extension of our personality (eg, a car). This extension of self concept theory in fact has been called symbolic interactionism because it Emphasises the interaction between individuals and the symbols in their environment.

Advertisers have understood the symbolic role of products in influencing self image. Advertising for jewellery, cosmetics, automobiles and clothing frequently communicates an image of the user.

Compared to other attitudes, the self-concept is a very complex structure. It is composed of many attributes, some of which are given greater emphasis in determining overall self-attitude. Attributes of self-concept can be described along such dimensions as their content (*e.g.*, facial attractiveness versus mental aptitude), positivity or negativity (*i.e.*, self-esteem), intensity, stability over time, and accuracy (*i.e.*, the degree to which one's self-assessment corresponds to reality). As will be seen later in the unit, consumers' self-assessments can be quite distorted, especially with regard to their physical appearance.

Q22.Explain the concept of self extension .

Ans. Those external objects that we consider a part of us comprise the extended self. In some cultures, people literally incorporate objects into the s(- they lick new possessions, take the names of conquered enemies (or in some cases eat them), or bury the dead with their possessions. Four levels of the extended self are used by consumers to define themselves. These range from very personal objects to places and thin, that allow people to feel like they are rooted in their environments.

- **Individual level:** Consumers include many of their personal possessions in self-definition. These products can include jewellery, cars, clothing, and so on. The saying "You are what you wear" reflects the belief that one's things are a part of what one is.
- **Family level:** This part of the extended self includes a consume's residence and the furnishings in it. The house can be thought of as a symbolic body of the family and is often a central aspect of identity.
- **Community level:** It is common for consumers to describe themselves in terms of the neighbourhood or town from which they come. For farm families or residents with close ties to a community, this sense of belonging is particularly important.
- **Group level:** Our attachments to certain social groups also can be considered a part of self. A consumer may feel that marks, landmarks, monuments, or sports teams are a part of the extended self.

Q23. The theory of cognitive dissonance is based on the premises that people have a need.

Ans. The strength of motive may not be very strong for the comfort or the discomfort of the marketer. This may be either because consumer are not aware of the importance of the buying decision or that the consumer make for themselves.

A purchase decision may involve more than one source of motivation. Consumers often find themselves in situations where different motives, both positive and negative, conflict with one another, since marketers are attempting to satisfy consumers' needs, they can also be helpful by providing possible solutions to these dilemmas. As shown in Figure, three general types of conflicts can occur: approach-approach, approach-avoidance, and avoidance-avoidance.

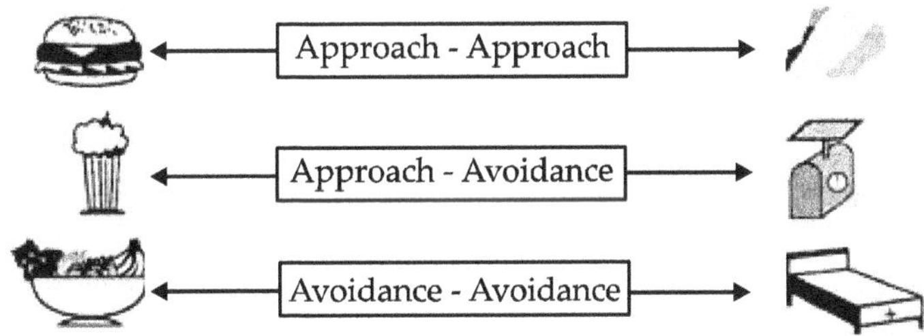

Approach-Approach Conflict: Here, a person must choose between two desirable alternative. A student might be torn between going home for the holidays or going on with friends for a sightseeing trip. Or, he or she might have to choose between two equally desired music albums but only one can be bought with the limited funds that they have.

Approach-Avoidance Conflict: Many of the product and services we desire have negative consequences attached to them as well. We may feel guilty or ostentatious when buying ice creams or expensive perfume. Some solutions to these conflicts include the proliferation of fake furs, which eliminate guilt about harming animals to make a fashion statement, and the success of diet foods, such as Weight Watchers, that promise good food without the calories. Many marketers try to overcome guilt by convincing consumers that they are deserving of luxuries.

The conflict of this kind gives rise to another consumer behaviour concept, called cognitive dissonance. The theory of cognitive dissonance is based on the premise that people have a need for order and consistency in their lives and that a state of tension is created when beliefs or behaviours conflict with one another. A state of dissonance occurs when there is a logical inconsistency between two or more beliefs or behaviours. It often occurs when a consumer must make a choice between two products, where both alternatives usually possess both good and bad qualities. By choosing one product and not the other, the person gets the bad qualities of the chosen product and loses out on the good qualities of the unchosen one. This loss creates an unpleasant, dissonant state that the person is motivated to reduce.

The conflict that arises when choosing between two alternatives may be resolved through a process of cognitive dissonance reduction, in which people are motivated to reduce this inconsistency (or dissonance) and thus, eliminate unpleasant tension. People tend to convince themselves after the fact that the choice they made was the smart one by finding additional reasons to support the alternative they chose, or perhaps by "discovering" flaws with the option they did not choose. A marketer can resolve an approach-avoidance conflict by bundling several benefits together. For example, Miller Lite's claim that it is "less filling" and "tastes great" allows the drinker to "have his beer and drink it too".

Avoidance–Avoidance Conflict: Sometimes consumers find themselves caught "between a rock and hard place." They may face a choice with two undesirable alternatives. A person may be faced with the option of either throwing more money into an old car or buying a new car. Marketers frequently address this conflict by message that stress the unforeseen benefits of choosing one option (*e.g.*, by Emphasising lease finance or easy payment plans to ease the pain of new-car payments). Similarly, the problem of remaining unemployed or taking up a job which is either life threatening or socially low. Medicine buying is another example of this type of conflict.

People may do things to satisfy motives of which they are not even aware. Human action is that each & every part if it s guided by motives or otherwise.

Q24.Illustrate the model of hypothesis values in buying a pressure cooker.

Ans. Stainless steel pressure cookers are nonporous, slightly heavier, and more expensive than aluminum models. The extremely durable nature of stainless steel will provide years of use with a beautiful high luster finish. However, by itself, stainless steel is not a good conductor of heat, so it's best to select a model with a layered base, usually a disc of aluminum bonded to the outside bottom of the pan. This will greatly improve the heating characteristics and performance of a stainless steel pressure cooker by eliminating "hot spots" that would otherwise be common in stainless steel cookware.

Size: Most pressure cookers are sold by the size of their total liquid capacity even though the actual usable capacity of a pressure cooker is one half to two thirds of its liquid capacity, depending upon the food being cooked. The extra space left in the cooker is necessary to allow steam to build inside the unit. Although, there are many sizes of pressure cookers in the marketplace, the most popular sizes are 4-, 6-, and 8-quart liquid capacities. We'll explore the advantages of these popular sizes to help you determine the best size for your needs.

Quart: A good size for singles or couples or for making one course for a family, such as potatoes or vegetables.

Brand name: Choose a brand from a company that has been in business for a number of years and has a stable financial track record. To keep your pressure cooker operating properly and safely for many years, you will have to periodically replace a few inexpensive parts (just as you would replace spark plugs and fan belts on your car). You need to be confident that the brand you purchase today will be from a company that will be in business for years to come in order to assure a supply of the proper parts. Parts are not interchangeable from one brand to another, so don't select a "brand X" model simply because it is less expensive. A closely related concept is the E-value, which is the average number of times in multiple testing that one expects to obtain a test statistic at least as extreme as the one that was actually observed, assuming that the null hypothesis is true. The E-value is the product of the number of tests and the p-value. In statistical significance testing, the p-value is the probability of obtaining a test statistic at least as extreme as the one that was actually observed, assuming that the null hypothesis is true. One often "rejects the null hypothesis" when the p-value is less than 0.05 or 0.01, corresponding respectively to a 5% or 1% chance of rejecting the null hypothesis when it is true .When the null hypothesis is rejected, the result is said to be statistically significant.

He practice of science involves formulating and testing hypotheses, assertions that are falsifiable using a test of observed data. The null hypothesis typically corresponds to a general or default position. For example, the null hypothesis might be that there is no relationship between two measured phenomena or that a potential treatment has no effect. Hypothesis testing works by collecting data and measuring how probable the data are, assuming the null hypothesis is true. If the data are very improbable (usually defined as observed less than 5% of the time), then the experimenter concludes that the null hypothesis is false. If the data do not contradict the null hypothesis, then no conclusion is made. In this case, the null hypothesis could be true or false; the data give insufficient evidence to make any conclusion. For instance, a certain drug may reduce the chance of having a heart attack. Possible null hypotheses are "this drug does not reduce the chances of having a heart attack" and "this drug has no effect on the chances of having a heart attack". The test of the hypothesis consists of administering the drug to half of the people in a study group as a controlled experiment. If the data show a statistically significant change in the people receiving the drug, the null hypothesis is rejected.

Q25. Illustrate the marketing response to the consumer attitude.

Ans. Customer behaviour study is based on consumer buying behaviour, with the customer playing the three distinct roles of user, payer and buyer. Relationship marketing is an influential asset for customer behaviour analysis as it has a keen interest in the re-discovery of the true meaning of marketing through the re-affirmation of the importance of the customer or buyer. A greater importance is also placed on consumer retention, customer relationship management, personalisation, customisation and one-to-one marketing. Social functions can be categorized into social choice and welfare functions.

Each method for vote counting is assumed as social function but if Arrow's possibility theorem is used for a social function, social welfare function is achieved. Some specifications of the social functions are decisiveness, neutrality, anonymity, monotonicity, unanimity, homogeneity and weak and strong Pareto optimality. No social choice function meets these requirements in an ordinal scale simultaneously. The most important characteristic of a social function is identification of the interactive effect of alternatives and creating a logical relation with the ranks. Marketing provides services in order to satisfy customers. With that in mind, the productive system is considered from its beginning at the production level, to the end of the cycle, the consumer. Consumer behaviour is the study of when, why, how, and where people do or do not buy a product. It blends elements from psychology, sociology, social anthropology and economics. It attempts to understand the buyer decision making process, both individually and in groups. It studies characteristics of individual consumers such as demographics and behavioural variables in an attempt to understand people's wants. It also tries to assess influences on the consumer from groups such as family, friends, reference groups, and society in general. Once the consumer has recognised a problem, they search for information on products and services that can solve that problem.

Sources of information include:

- Personal sources.
- Commercial sources
- Public sources
- Personal experience

The relevant internal psychological process that is associated with information search is perception. Perception is defined as "the process by which an individual receives, selects, organises, and interprets information to create a meaningful picture of the world".

The selective perception process

Stage Description

- Selective exposure consumers select which promotional messages they will expose themselves to.
- Selective attention consumers select which promotional messages they will pay attention to.
- Selective comprehension consumer interpret messages in line with their beliefs, attitudes, motives and experiences.

- Selective retention consumers remember messages that are more meaningful or important to them.

The implications of this process help develop an effective promotional strategy, and select which sources of information are more effective for the brand. Once the alternatives have been evaluated, the consumer is ready to make a purchase decision. Sometimes purchase intention does not result in an actual purchase. The marketing organisation must facilitate the consumer to act on their purchase intention. The organisation can use variety of techniques to achieve this. The provision of credit or payment terms may encourage purchase, or a sales promotion such as the opportunity to receive a premium or enter a competition may provide an incentive to buy now. The relevant internal psychological process that is associated with purchase decision is integration. Once the integration is achieved, the organisation can influence the purchase decisions much more easily. Consumer behaviour is influenced by: demographics, psychographics (lifestyle), personality, motivation, knowledge, attitudes, beliefs, and feelings. Consumer behaviour concern with consumer need consumer actions in the direction of satisfying needs leads to his behaviour of every individuals depend on thinking. Consumer behaviour is influenced by: culture, sub-culture, locality, royalty, ethnicity, family, social class, past experience reference groups, lifestyle, market mix factors.

Q26. Is it possible to assist the retrieval of information from the memory?

Ans. Retrieval is the process whereby information is accessed from long-term memory. As evidenced by the popularity of the game Business (Monopoly), people have a vast quantity of information stored in their heads that is not necessarily available on demand. Although most of the information entered in long-term memory does not go away, it may be hard or impossible to retrieve unless the appropriate cues are present.

- **Pictorial versus Verbal Cues:** There is some evidence for the superiority of visual memory over verbal memory, but this advantage is unclear because it is more difficult to measure recall of pictures. However, the available data indicate that information presented in picture form is more likely to be recognised later certainly, visual aspects of an ad are more likely to grab a consumer's attention. In fact, eye-movement studies indicate that about 90 per cent of viewers look at the dominant picture in an ad before they bother to view the copy. One study found that television news items presented with illustration (still pictures) as a backdrop result in improved recall for details of the new story, even though understanding of the story's content does not improve.

- **Familiarity:** As a general rule, prior familiarity with an item enhances its recall. Indeed, this is one of the basic goals of marketers who are trying to create and maintain awareness of their products. The more experience a consumer has with a product, the better use he or she is able to make of product information. However, there is a possible exception to the rule. Evidence indicates that extreme familiarity can result in inferior learning and/or recall. When consumers are highly familiar with a brand or an advertisement, they may attend to fewer attributes because they do not believe that any additional effort will yield a gain in knowledge. For example, when consumers are exposed to the technique of radio replay, where the audio track from a television ad is replayed on the radio, they do very little critical, evaluative processing and instead mentally replay the video portion of the ad.
- **Salience:** The salience of a brand refers to its prominence or level of activation in memory. Stimuli that stand out in contrast to their environment are more likely to command attention, which in turn, increases the likelihood they will be recalled. Almost any technique that increases the novelty of a stimulus also improves recall (a result known as the von Restorff effect). This effect explains why unusual advertising or distinctive packaging tend to facilitate brand recall.
- **State-Dependent Retrieval:** In a process termed state-dependent retrieval, people are better able to access information if their internal state is the same at the time of recall as when the information was learned. This phenomenon is called the mood congruence effect. The fact underscores the desirability of matching a consumer's mood at the time of purchase when planning exposure to marketing communications. A consumer is more likely to recall an ad, for example, if his or her mood or level of arousal at the time of exposure is similar to that in the purchase environment. By recreating the cues that were present when the information was first presented, recall can be enhanced. For example, Parle G uses a picture of "Mile bottle on its packaging as well as the advertisement. It intends to facilitate recall of brand claims and favouurable brand evaluations.
- **Factors Influencing Retrieval:** Some differences in retrieval ability are physiological. Older adults consistently display inferior recall ability for current items such as prescription information, though events that happened to them why they were younger may be recalled with great clarity. Other factors are situational, relating to the environment in which the message is delivered. Not surprisingly recall is enhanced

when the consumer pays more attention to the message in the first place. Some evidence indicates that information about a pioneering brand (the first brand to enter a market) is more easily retrieved from memory than follower brands because the product's introduction is likely to be distinctive and, for the time being, no competitors divert the consumer's attention. In addition, descriptive brand names are more likely to be recalled than are those that do not provide adequate cues as to what the product is.

Q27. Assist the measuring the memory for advertising.

Ans. Learning is change in behaviour that is caused by experience. Learning can occur through simple associations between a stimulus and a response, or a via a complex series of cognitive activities. Behavioural learning theories assume that learning occurs as a result of responses to external events. Classical conditioning occurs when a stimulus that naturally elicits a response is paired with another stimulus that does not initially elicits the response. The goal is to not just keep your audience engaged on a regular basis, but to provide grist for the search engines to bring relevant traffic to your site. And good content has a habit of being passed around on social media sites.

(1) Recognition versus Recall: One indicator of good advertising is, of course, the impression it makes on consumers. But how can this impact be defined and measured? Two basic measures of impact are recognition and recall. In the typical recognition test, subjects are shown ads one at a time and asked if they have seen them before. In contrast, free recall tests ask consumers to independently produce previously acquired information and then perform a recognition check on it. Under some conditions, these two memory measures tend to yield the same results, especially when the researchers try to keep the viewers' interest in the ads constant. Generally, though, recognition scores tend to be more reliable and do not decay over time the way recall scores do. Recognition scores are almost always better than recall scores because recognition is a simpler process and more retrieval cues are available to the consumer.

Both types of retrieval play important roles in purchase decisions. Recall tests tend to be more important in situations where consumers do not have product data at their disposal, and so they must rely upon memory to generate this information. On the other hand, recognition is more likely to be an important factor in a store, where consumers are confronted with thousands of product options and information (*i.e.*, external memory is abundantly available) and the task may simply be to recognise a familiar package. For example, the Maharajah of the Air India icon is quickly recognised by all consumers.

(2) Problems with Memory Measures: While the measurement of an ad's memorability is important, the ability of existing measures to accurately assess these dimensions has been criticized for several reasons.

(i) Response Biases: Results obtained from a measuring instrument are not necessarily due to what is being measured, but rather to something else about the instrument or the respondent. This form of contamination is called a response bias. For example, people tend to give yes responses to questions, regardless of what is asked. In addition, consumers often have an eagerness to be "good subjects" by pleasing the experimenter. They will try to give the responses they think he or she is looking for. In some studies, the claimed recognition of bogus ads (ads that have not been seen before) is almost as high as the recognition rate of real ads.

(ii) Memory Lapses: Typical problems include omitting (leaving facts out), averaging (the tendency to "normalize" things and not report extreme cases), and telescoping (inaccurate recall of time). These distortions call into question the accuracy of various product usage data bases that rely upon consumers to recall their purchase and consumption of food and household items. In one study, for example, people were asked to describe what portion of various foods-small, medium, or large they ate in a normal meal. However, different definitions of medium were used (*e.g.*, 3/4 cup versus cups). Regardless of the measurement used, about the same number of people claimed they normally ate medium portions.

(iii) Memory versus Feeling: Although techniques are being developed to increase the. accuracy of memory scores, these improvements do not address the more fundamental issue of whether recall is necessary for advertising to have an effect. In particular, some critics argue that these measures do not adequately, tap the impact of "feeling" ads where the objective is to arouse strong emotions rather than to convey concrete product benefits. Many ads campaigns, including those for Hallmark cards, Chevrolet, and Pepsi use this approach. An effective strategy relies on a long-term buildup of feeling rather than on a one-shot attempt to convince consumers to buy the product.

(3) The Starch Test: A widely used commercial measure of advertising recall for magazines is called the Starch test, a syndicated service founded in 1932. This service provides scores on a number of aspects of consumers' familiarity with an ad, including such categories as "noted," "associated," and "read most." It also scores the impact of the component parts of an overall ad, giving such information as "seen" for major illustrations and "read some" for a major block of copy. Such factors as the size of the ad, whether it appears toward the front or the back of magazine, if it is on the right or left page, and the size of illustrations play an important role in affecting the amount of attention given to an ad as determined by Starch scores. The ad for Whittle Communications highlights the problem of consumers noticing ads and processing them for recall and retrieval.

Q28. Define the marketing applications.

Ans. When there are multiple versions of a product, the company often forgets to include a comparison chart on its website; when there is a chart, it usually compares features not benefits, making the chart useless. Observing learning takes place when the consumer performs a behaviour as result of seeing someone else performing it and being rewarded for it.

Repetition: The first creates awareness of the product, the second demonstrates its relevance to the consumer, and the third serves as a reminder of the product's benefits. However, even this bare-bones approach implies that repetition is needed to ensure that the consumer is actually exposed to (and processes) the ad at least three times. Marketers attempting to condition an association must ensure that the consumers they have targeted will be exposed to the stimulus a sufficient number of times.

On the other hand, it is possible to have too much of a good thing: Consumers can become so used to hearing or seeing a marketing stimulus that they no longer pay attention to it. This problem, known as advertising wear out, can be alleviated by varying the way in which the basic message is presented.

Conditioning Product Associations: Advertisements often pair a product with a positive stimulus to create a desirable association. Various aspects of a marketing message, such as music, humor, or imagery, can affect conditioning. In one study, for example, subjects who viewed a slide of pens paired with either pleasant or unpleasant music were more likely to later select the pen that appeared with pleasant music. The order in which the conditioned stimulus and the unconditioned stimulus is presented can affect the likelihood that learning will occur. Generally speaking, the conditioned stimulus should be presented prior to the unconditioned stimulus. The technique of conditioning, such showing a soft drink (the UCS) and then playing a jingle (the CS) is generally not effective. Because sequential presentation is desirable for conditioning to occur, classical conditioning is not very effective in static situations, such as in magazine ads, where (in contrast to TV or radio) the marketer cannot control the order in which the CS and the UCS are perceived.

Just as product associations can be formed, they can extinguished. Because of the danger of extinction, a classical conditioning strategy may not be as effective for products that are frequently encountered, since there is no guarantee they will be accompanied by the CS. A bottle of Pepsi paired with the refreshing sound of a carbonated beverage being poured over ice may seem like a good example of conditioning. Unfortunately, the product would also be seen in many other contexts where this sound was absent, reducing the effectiveness of the conditioning.

By the same reasoning, a novel tune should be chosen over a popular one to pair with a product, since the popular song might also be heard in many situations where the product is not present. Music videos in particular may serve as effective UCSs because they often have an emotional impact on viewers, and this effect may transfer to ads accompanying the video.

Stimulus Generalization: The process of stimulus generalization is often central to branding and packaging decisions that attempt to capitalize on consumers' positive associations with an existing brand or company name. In one twenty-month period, Proctor & Gamble introduced almost ninety new products. Not a single one carried a new brand name. Infact, roughly 80 per cent of all new products are actually extensions of existing brands or product lines. Strategies based on stimulus generalization include the following.

- **Family branding,** where a variety of products capitalize on the reputation of a company name. Companies such as Maggi's rely on their positive corporate images to sell different product lines.
- **Product line extensions,** where related products are added to an established brand. Captain Cook, which is associated with salt, has been able to introduce wheat flour, spices etc. under the same brand name.
- **Licensing,** where well-known names are "rented" by others. This strategy is increasing in popularity as marketers try to link their products and services with well-established figures. The Disney Characters and the companies as diverse as McDonald's have authorized the use of their names on products.
- **Look-alike packaging,** where distinctive packaging designs create strong associations with a particular brand. This linkage often is exploited by makers of generic or private-label brands who wish to communicate a quality image by putting their products in very similar packages.
- **Reinforcement of Consumption.** Marketers have many ways to reinforce consumers, ranging from a simple thank you after a purchase

to sub-stantial rebates and follow-up phone calls. For example, a life insurance company obtained a much higher rate of policy renewal among a group of new customers who received a thank you letter after each payment compared to a control group that did not receive any rein- forcement.

Q29. Mention the key words of psychoanalytic and the social theories of personality and compare them together.

Or

State the Neo-freudian theory.

Ans. Some social-psychologists have forwarded the view that, social relationships are fundamental to the formations and development of personality. On the basis of their orientations in relating to others, individual consumers tend to develop methods to cope with their anxieties, Consumers have consequently been classified into three personality groups using what is called the 'CAD model' where CAD is an acronym that stands for compliance, aggression and detachment. The CAD model was developed by using the concept of `interpersonal man' and considers all consumers as having one of three basic orientations so that they may be described as belonging to one of the following categories of individuals:

- **Compliant Individuals:** These individuals tend to move toward others. Compliant people have a need for love, affection, approval and the desire to be appreciated. They are essentially conformists.
- **Aggressive Individuals:** They tend to move against others. Their interpersonal orientations display the ability to manipulate others. Such individuals also appear to have a need to achieve success, to excel, to gain admiration and to be in a power position.
- **Detached Individuals:** This category of persons tend to move away from others. Their relationships emphaise the need for self-reliance, independence, and freedom.

Application of Social-psychological Theory: It has been found that individuals having different personality types tend to use different products and brands. The CAD model was, in fact, developed for the specific purpose of studying buying behaviour and it emphasises the effect of social influences on the personality. Thus, studies have shown that compliant types have been found to prefer known products and brands while aggressive types have been found to prefer specific brands out of a desire to be noticed, and also to use more of aftershave lotions and colognes. In contrast, detached types appear to have the least awareness of brands. The CAD approach is used by marketers to predict which consumers may be more or less prone to group influence.

The most important application of social-psychological theory is its emphasis on the social nature of consumption. In fact you will see this in advertising copy in which social interaction is stressed more than the products themselves. Advertising for personal care products, for instance, emphasises the fear of offending others. Social interaction is also highlighted in the case of products advertised for occasions for being together.

Q30. Explain the concept of symbolic interactionism.

Ans. Symbolic interactionism : The self is a basic concept in symbolic interactionism. The essential feature of the self is that it is a reflexive phenomenon. Reflexivity enables humans to act toward themselves as objects, or to reflect on themselves, argue with themselves, evaluate themselves, and so forth. This human attribute (al-though dolphins and the great apes show some evidence of a self as well), based on the social character of human language and the ability to role-take, enables individuals to see themselves from the perspective of another and thereby to form a conception of themselves, a self-concept. The self is considered a social product in other ways, too. The content of self-concepts reflects the content and organisation of society. This is evident with regard to the roles that are internalized as role-identities (*e.g.*, father, student). Roles, as behavioural expectations associated with a status within a set of relationships, constitute a major link between social and personal organisation. Sheldon Stryker (1980) proposes that differential commitment to various role-identities provides much of the structure and organisation of self-concepts. To the extent that individuals are committed to a particular role identity, they are motivated to act according to their conception of the identity and to maintain and protect it, because their role performance implicates their self-esteem. Much of socialisation, particularly during childhood, involves learning social roles and associated values, attitudes, and beliefs. Initially this takes place in the family, then in larger arenas (*e.g.*, peer groups, school, work settings) of the individual's social world. The role identities formed early in life, such as gender and filial identities, remain some of the most important throughout life. Yet socialisation is lifelong, and individuals assume various role identities throughout their life course.

If each person potentially has many social selves, how does each develop and how do we decide which self to "activate" at any point in time? The sociological tradition of symbolic Interactionism stresses that relationships with other people play a part informing the self. This perspective maintains that people exist in a symbolic environment and the meaning attached to any situation or object is determined by the interpretation of these symbols. As members of society, we learn to agree on shared meanings. Thus, we know that a red light means stop, the "golden arches" means fast food etc. etc.

Like other social objects, the meanings of consumers themselves are defined by social consensus. The consumer interprets his or her own identity, and this assessment is continually evolving as he or she encounters new situations and people. In symbolic interactionist terms, we negotiate these meanings over time. Essentially the consumer poses the question: "Who am I in this situation?" The answer to this question is greatly influenced by those around us: "Who do other people think I am?" We tend to pattern our behaviour on the perceived expectations of others in a form of self-fulfilling prophecy. By acting the way we assume others expect us to act, we wind up confirming these perception.

Socialisation is not a passive process of learning roles and conforming to other's expectations. The self is highly active and selective, having a major influence on its environment and itself. When people play roles, role-making often is as evident as is learning roles. In role-making, individuals actively construct, interpret, and uniquely express their roles. When they perceive an incongruity between a role imposed on them and some valued aspect of their self-conception, they may distance themselves from a role, which is the disassociation of self from role. A pervasive theme in this literature is that the self actively engages in its own development, a process that may be unpredictable.

Q31. Explain the concept of Self-consciousness & self-esteem.

Ans. In role-making, individuals actively construct, interpret, and uniquely express their roles. When they perceive an incongruity between a role imposed on them and some valued aspect of their self-conception, they may distance themselves from a role, which is the disassociation of self from role. A pervasive theme in this literature is that the self actively engages in its own development, a process that may be unpredictable.

Self-Consciousness: Unlike the feeling in self concept, self consciousness is more deliberate and easily felt or told. Thus, there are times when people seem to be painfully aware of themselves. If you have ever walked into a class in the middle of lecture and noticed that all eyes were on you, you can understand this feeling of self consciousness. In contrast, consumers sometimes behave with little self-consciousness. For example, people may do things in a stadium, a riot, or a fraternity party that they would never do if they were highly conscious of their behaviour.

In the marketing consumption context, some products do bring out self consciousness in the customers while they are buying or considering them. Thus, `esteem' products or the `unmentionable products' make the customers very self conscious of them. The rule of the thumb in this regard is that if a person is doing what he or she is not supposed to do in the normal course, it makes them conscious of themselves: It is both a marketing opportunity and a challenge.

Self Esteem: Self-esteem refers to the 'positivity of one's attitude toward oneself'. People with low self-esteem do not expect that they will perform very well. They thus, constantly endeavour to avoid embarrassment, failure, or rejection. In developing a new line of snack cakes, for example, a manufacturer found that consumers low in self-esteem, preferred portion controlled snack items because they felt they lacked self-control. In contrast, people with high self-esteem expect to be successful, will take more risks, and are more willing to be the center of attention.

Self-esteem often is related to acceptance by others. For example, young persons who move in high-status "crowds in the disco bars" have higher self-esteem than their counterparts. Like the situation in the self consciousness, the self esteem too poses an opportunity to the marketers. Some products could be employing the self esteem angle to project their products. Citicards have used this approach for making their cards more acceptable. Similarly, the new campaign of the new Lifebouy personal soap has used how the brand gives a lift to self esteem of those who are not confident of themselves or have a lower self-esteem.

3

Group Influences on Consumer Behaviour

Q1. What do you mean by a Reference Group?

Or

What is a reference group? What type of influences exerted from normative and comparative reference groups?

Or

Write a short note on Reference Group.

Ans. Within the context of consumer behaviour, the concept of reference groups is an extremely important and powerful idea. A reference group is any person or group that serves as a point of comparison (or reference) for an individual in forming either general or specific values, attitudes, or a specific guide for behaviour. This basic concept provides a valuable perspective for understanding the impact of other people on an individual's consumption beliefs, attitudes, and behaviour. It also provides insight into the methods marketers sometimes use to effect desired changes in consumer behaviour. From a marketing perspective, reference groups are groups that serve as frames of reference for individuals in their purchase or consumption decisions. The usefulness of this concept is enhanced by the fact that it places no restrictions on group size or membership, nor does it require that consumers identify with a tangible group (*i.e.,* the group can be symbolic such as owners of successful small businesses, leading corporate chief executive officers, country music stars, or baseball celebrities).

The influence exerted by the group depends on the type of reference group it is.

Normative Reference Groups: These are group whose values, norms and perspective an individual uses in defining a personal social situation. Norms represent shared value judgements about how things should be done by members of the group. For example, dress codes indicate the impact of normative influence on clothing. Similarly, norms influence how much a person eats or drinks at a party.

Normative influence refers to the influence exerted by a group to conform to its norms and behaviour. A group can exert normative influence in the purchase of clothes, furniture and appliances because these items are visible. Normative influence may also occur for items like mouthwash, even though such items are not visible, because of fear of punishment of non-acceptance by the group. However, normative influence is not likely to occur for products like vegetables, though informational influence could occur in such cases. Since normative influence is based on the desire of an individual to receive the rewards of the group, the influence exerted by the group in such is also termed as utilitarian influence.

Comparative Reference Groups: Consumers constantly compare their attitudes to those of members of their important groups. In doing this, they seek to support their own attitudes and behaviour. As a result, the basis for comparative influence is the process of comparing oneself to other members of the group and judging whether it will be supportive. You will find that new residents in a neighbourhood are attracted to neighbours who are similar to themselves because they reinforce existing attitudes and behaviour. You will also find this in advertising that uses spokespersons whom consumers perceive as being similar to themselves.

The function of comparative reference groups is to provide a basis for validating beliefs, values, and attitudes. Furthermore, in terms of reference group theory, it is not necessary for consumers to be in direct social contact with a reference group in order to be influenced by it.

In the case of comparative reference groups, value-expressive influence occurs when the group is used to express certain values. For example, smoking cigarettes in reference groups where it is okay to smoke, is a type of value expressive influence. In fact, expressing the values of the group is a good way to become accepted by the group and form a close association with it.

Q2. What factors are important in reference group influence on buying decisions?

Ans. Reference groups' influence is accepted and sought by individuals because of the perceived benefits that it provides. Thus, the interaction may result in rewards of friendship, information and satisfaction. However, the degree of influence that a reference group exerts on an individual's behavior depends on several factors.

- **How Informed and Experienced the Individual is:** A person who has little or no first-hand experience with a product or service, and also little or no information, will tend to rely on reference groups. Where there is insufficient experience or information, a consumer is more susceptible to the influence of others.
- **Reference Group Credibility:** The higher a reference group is rated on credibility, the more powerful it will be perceived to be, and the more it will tend to change the beliefs, attitudes and behavior of consumers. Also, the more it will be used for information on product quality.

Q3. In what ways the reference group influences on both product and brand decision?

Ans. Individual often buy particular brands because they observe others buying them, and not necessarily in order to comply with group behaviour. At social gatherings too, people discuss at lengths, products they like and dislike, recounting personal experiences with products they have used. It is necessary to consider carefully, therefore, how much influence reference groups are likely to have for a product or service. Those products or services that have strong group usage or connotation should then be presented in a group context in advertising situations.

- **Influence on Product and Brand** (Public Luxuries): Certain groups are more likely to allow smoking, than others. If smoking is the norm, the group is likely to express a preference for a certain brand. Reference group influence is Therefore,likely to be strong for both the product and the brand.
- **Influence on Product only** (Private Luxuries): Some product categories are so distinctive that owing them is sufficiently representative of group standards, for example, air conditioners, and home computers. Once a family buys a home computer, for instance, friends and neighbours will come into contact with the recently acquired product and the pattern of ownership will spread within the group.
- **Influence on Brand only** (Public Necessities): There are some products that are used by almost everyone. For example, clothing, furniture, magazines, toilet soaps. In such cases, the product is not subject to group influence. The brand becomes an important factor subject to group influence. Thus, one group may emphasise designer clothes as a distinguishing feature. Another may emphasise leisure wear. Another group may read high brow magazines as the norm.

- **No Group Influence** (Private Necessities): Some products have low social visibility for both the product and the brand. In such cases reference group influence is weak or absent. Such products are then bought on the basis of product attributes suitable to the consumer. Products low in visibility, complexity and perceived risk such as bread, are not likely to be susceptible to personal influence.

Q4. Categorize the social class.

Ans. Money creates class distinctions. Enough money makes you wealthy or rich and not enough makes you working class or poor. Though both classes share the same planet they live in different worlds. The wealthy can afford the best of everything while the poor or working class struggle to keep a roof overhead and food on the table. While the lower class may consider the upper class to be snobs and undeserving of their wealth the upper class consider them to be their social inferiors.

Identification of members within each social class is influenced most heavily by education and occupation, including income, as a measure of work success. But it is also affected by family recreational habits and social acceptance by a particular class. Thus, social class is a composite of many personal and social attributes rather than a single characteristic such as income or education.

Traditionally, social class positioning has been measured in terms of socio-economic factors, namely, type and source of income (inheritance or salary), occupational status, level of education, value of housing and quality of neighboured. Socio-economic factors appeal to marketers because the information is easily collected as part of any questionnaire. It is Thus,possible to prepare profiles of the potential target markets.

The number of categories of social class varies. They are ordered in a manner that begins with some type of elite upper class and ends with a lower class. A variety of different classification schemes has been developed, to rank the social classes. A frequently used scheme is the well known Warner's Index of Status Characteristics (ISC).

Warner's Index uses four variables as indicators of social class. They are occupation, income; house and dwelling area. Warner categorised the members in a society into six classes as follows:

- Upper-upper class
- Lower-upper class
- Upper-middle class
- Lower-middle class
- Upper-lower class

- Lower-lower class

The percentage of population accounted for in each social class appears to fluctuate but is concentrated in the middle and lower classes. The concept of mass marketing can, for instance, be applied to the middle classes but not to the affluent upper-upper. The upper-upper is, however, a desirable target market for speciality goods marketing by firms. Such goods can appeal to the cultivated tastes of a very small number of affluent consumers.

The social classes are described for marketing purposes, in terms of the social groups from which they are drawn in society. On the basis of demographic factors we Thus,have:

- **The upper-upper social class:** This is the wealthy, aristocratic, landed class. It serves as a reference for the social classes below. It is not a major market segment, because of its small size.
- **The lower-upper social class:** This is the newer social elite. Money is relatively new. It is an achieving group, drawn from professionals and, includes the successful and wealthy executive elite, doctors, lawyers and founders of large businesses. It constitutes a major market for specialised luxury goods.
- **The upper-middle class:** This class consists of the moderately successful. It consists of the professionally educated managers, intellectual elite and successful professionals, doctors, lawyers, and professors, owners of medium-sized businesses and managerial executives, and also younger men and women who are expected to reach these occupational status levels. Housing is important to this class, and also the appearance of products in general.
- **The lower-middle class:** It is represented by the common man, and the highly paid individual worker. It includes the small business owners and non-managerial workers. Persons in this class tend to have high school educations and some college education, but do not reach high levels in their organisations.
- **The working class:** This is the largest of the social classes, and is composed of skilled and semi-skilled workers.

They are blue (Khaki) collar workers but have sufficient money for consumer products, and along with the middle classes, they represent the market for mass consumer goods.

Q5. Do you think that social class would be a better predictor of consumer lifestyles than income?

Ans. Social class has Thus,been found better than income for expressive types of consumer behaviour such as private club membership, ownership of farm houses, type of automobile owned, type of stores patronised, and also the particular brands purchased. It is Therefore,necessary that, promotional messages, distribution channels and, retail outlets be effectively related to social class membership. However, social class has not always been successful in segmenting markets, and there has been a long controversy as to whether social class or income is a better variable for segmentation. The choice between the two appears to depend on the product and the situation. Social class variable has been found superior to income variable for the purchase of highly visible symbols and expensive objects such as living room furnishings. What is important for market segmentation is that, within each social class, there will be similarly shared values, attitudes and behaviour patterns. Income has been found to be a better predictor for major kitchen and laundry appliances and products that require substantial expenditure but are not status symbols. lastly, the combination of social class and income have been found superior for product classes that are visible, serve as symbols of social status and require moderate expenditure like television sets, cars and clothing.

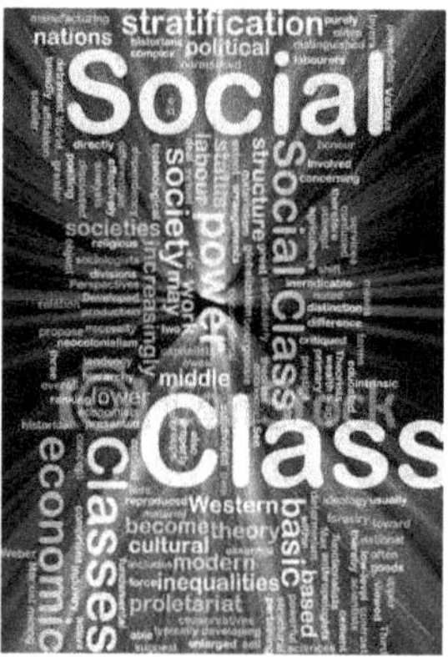

Fig. 3.1: Social Class

Q6. Discuss the nature and types of influences of family buying behaviour.

Ans. Family buying behaviour has been researched extensively. Companies are also interested in which family members have the most influence over certain purchases.

The family is not just a social group. It is also an earning, consuming, decision-making unit, and it is of importance to marketers because of the influence that family members have on purchase and consumption decision.

The family's influence comes from the fact that the bonds within the family are likely to be much more powerful and intimate than those in other small groups. Because of these bonds, the family has profound social, cultural, psychological, and economic influence on consumers. Within the family, operating as the unit of analysis, a reciprocal influence operates on all decisions. There are three main sources of influence in the family decision process. These are the father, the mother, and other family members.

Since a particular family may have several persons in the 'other family members' category, the decision process for a given family can be complex. Every family member brings his or her own motives, evaluations, beliefs and predispositions to the decision process. Every family member becomes part of the environment for the other family members and, influences, and is influenced by them. And the cognitions, behaviour and environments of the several persons become an important consideration for the marketer, as do the interactions of the members among themselves.

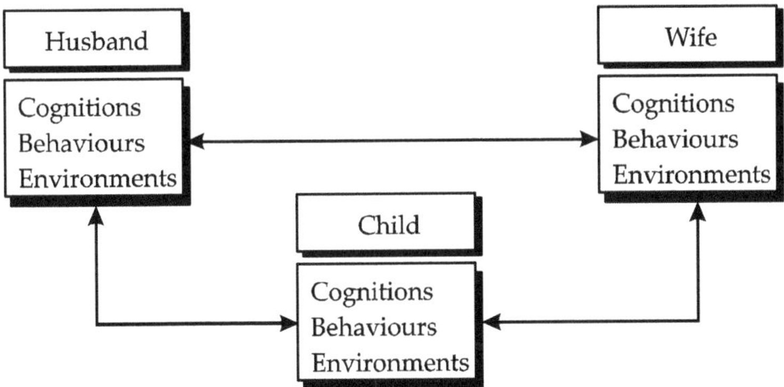

Fig. 3.2: The Reciprocal Influence of Family Members

Q7. Identify the family role structure and buying behaviour. Describe the family decision stages.

Ans. Purchase roles or tasks are assigned and carried out by one or more family members. When trying to reach families, therefore, marketers need to realise that a set of purchase roles exist and come into play within the family. These roles can be identified and they determine how families make decisions.

The important buying roles include:

(1) The Instigator (Initiator): This is the person who first suggests the idea of a product or service and initiates the purchase process, to begin with. The Initiator can even be a stranger.For example, you may see someone walking down the street, wearing a new style of sweater or shirt, and decide that you would like a similar one.

(2) The Influencer: This is someone whose opinion is valued in the decision-making process. An influencer may be a friend, brother, sister, spouse, doctor or other influential person. All these persons have a direct or indirect influence on the final purchase decision.

(3) The Decider: This is the person who makes the final decision on what brand or make to buy, after all aspects such as price, quality, servicing, have been thought over.

(4) The Purchaser (Buyer): This is the individual who actually purchases the product, pays for it, takes it home or arranges for delivery. Very often, the purchaser and the decider are the same person, particularly for big value items.

(5) The Consumer: He is the user of the goods or service.

Although these five buying roles are performed whenever a purchase is made, the individual performing each role may vary from purchase to purchase, and from family to family. The number and identity of the family members who fill these roles Thus,varies. In any given situation, the same member may take on several or all roles. Thus, in some cases, a single family member may independently assume a number of roles, in which case, it is really an individual decision within a family context. In other cases, a single role will be performed jointly by two or more family members. Multiple roles, too, may be performed by one of the family members. For example, in the purchase of household cleaning products, a single person may performhg all buying roles. In contrast, in purchasing cornflakes, the mother may act as the decider and buyer, her children as influencers and users and her husband as the evaluator. Thus, different persons may perform different tasks in the purchase process. In all cases, family roles are usually appointed in a way that ensures that they will be handled efficiently.

Family Decision Stages: Just as there are different purchase roles, there are also a number of different steps in the decision to buy a product or service. And the amount of influence exerted by the husband, wife and children will vary, depending on the stage of the decision process. The simplest of these is the five-stage decision-making model which includes:

(1) Problem recognition

(2) Search for information

(3) Evaluation of alternatives

(4) Final decision

(5) Purchase

The role of husband, wife and children will differ across the stages. There can Thus,be shifts in the husband-wife decision-making from stage one of problem recognition, to stage two of search for information and finally, to the decision. Marketers should Therefore,examine husband-wife decision-making in terms of specific purchase factors.

Q8. What are the dynamics of husband-wife decision-making?

Ans. Marketers are interested in the relative amount of influence that a husband and a wife have when it comes to family consumption choices. The relative influence of husbands and wife can be classified as: husband dominated, wife dominated, joint, and autonomic.

The relative influence of a husband and wife on a particular consumer decision depends in part on the product and service category. For instance, during the 1950s, the purchase of a new automobile was strongly husband dominated whereas food and financial banking decision more often were wife dominated. Fifty years later, the purchase of the family's principal automobile is still often husband dominated in many households. However, in other contexts or situations (e.g. a car to transport the children around or a car for a working mother), female car buyers are a segment to which many car manufacturers are currently receiving a great deal of marketing attention. Also, in the case of financial decision-making, there has been a general trend over the past decade to have the female head of household make financial decisions.

Husband-wife decision-making also appears to be related to cultural influence. Research comparing husband-wife decision-making patterns in the People's Republic of China and in the United States reveals that among Chinese there were substantially fewer "joint" decision and more "husband-dominated" decisions for many household purchases. However, when limiting the comparison to urban and rural Chinese households (i.e. a "within-Chine" comparison), the research showed that in a larger city such as Beijing, married couples were more likely than rural couples to share equally in purchase decisions. Still further, because of China's "one child" policy and the ensuing custom of treating a single child as a "little emperor", many of the parents' purchase decisions are influenced by the input of their child.

In another recent cross-cultural study, husband-wife decision-making was studied among three groups: Asian Indians living in India, Asian Indians living in the United States, and American nationals. Results show a decrease in husband-dominated decisions and an increase in wife-dominated decision, going from Asian Indians in India, to Asian Indians in the United States, to American nationals. This pattern seems to indicate the impact of assimilation on decision-making.

Q9. Explain the family life cycle concept.

Ans. The concept of a family life cycle was crucially linked to the nuclear family, the events of marriage and childbearing, and a presumed continuity of membership. Later social scientists broadened the definitions of the family and its phases and avoided restrictive or normative definitions that require formal marriage or childbearing. Many individuals never marry, many couples never have children, and many couples divorce and remarry with or without children. It is common to encompass these broad variations under the rubric of the life course, rather than the life cycle, for families as well as for individuals. The concept of the life cycle was originally developed for individuals and was then extended to an aggregate, the family, in influential articles published in the 1930s. Thus, the term family life cycle refers to the series of life stages through which individuals proceed over time. It describes, in other words, the process of family formation and dissolution.

The life cycle of families has been conceptualized as a progression involving several stages:

(1) The Bachelor Stage (Young and single): In the bachelor stage of the life cycle, income is low relative to future earnings, since most bachelors are just beginning their careers. However, there are few financial burdens. They Therefore,have relatively high discretionary incomes. They tend to spend substantial amounts on personal consumption items, food, clothing, transportation, certain luxury goods, entertainment, vacations, and possibly even a car. A few basic furniture items may be acquired, as well as some kitchen equipment. However,these purchases tend to be on a non-systematic basis and also minimal, because possessions restrict their freedom of movement.

(2) The Newly Married Couples (Young, no children): With marriage, the requirements and resources change. Household requirements increase. In addition, in some cases, both partners may be working. This stage therefore represents a high expenditure period. Purchases include durable goods such as refrigerators and other appliances, inexpensive durable furniture, home entertainment items such as TV sets. These items often take priority over other purchases.

(3) Full Nest 1 (Young, married, with child): The arrival of a child creates major changes. Some wives may stop working and they suffer a reduction in income. The financial resources Thus,change significantly. Child rearing and educational responsibilities increase. Money is now directed to baby furniture, toys, chest rubs, vitamins, baby foods, and baby medicines. While more shopping is done, the family also faces more medical bills. This is also the period that they become dissatisfied with their income and with their inability to accumulate earnings.

(4) Full Nest 2 (Older, married, with children): The family's financial position starts to improve because of career progress and also because many wives return to work. They present an active market for a wide variety of food products, bicycles, music lessons, magazines and also educational services as children are growing up.

(5) Full Nest 3 (Older, married, with dependent children): Income is high for the family at this stage. However, they now represent experienced buyers and tend to be less interested in new product purchases. Expenditures continue to be high due to replacement buying in the later phases of the stage.

(6) Empty Nest (Older, married, with no children living with them) : With no children living at home, the financial position stabilises. Savings accumulate. There may be a resurgence in self-education. Hobbies also become an important source of satisfaction. More is spent on luxury appliances, magazines and health products. Major expenditures are on home ownership, home improvements and also on medical care.

(7) Solitary Survivor (Older, single, retired people): Simple, often more economical lifestyle. A lower income due to retirement may be a restrictive factor. Health care and other services become important.

The stages at which families find themselves Thus,affect the nature of the goods and services required, their wants and consumption patterns, as well as the volume of consumption on specific products. At each stage there are unique needs, different patterns of object accumulation, and different demands that are placed on the family.

It would seem, therefore, that the family life cycle is a better predictor of consumption patterns than age. For example, it is well known that major furniture items are bought at or shortly after marriage, regardless of age. Conversely, furniture purchases tend to be put off in favouur of baby furniture and medical expenses at the time and stage required.

Q10. What are the implications of family decision-making for marketing strategy?

Ans. Once it is recognised that the same individual may not perform all the purchase consumption tasks, it becomes clear that the development of a successful marketing mix depends on answers to questions such as:

(1) Is the product likely to be purchased for joint or family use?

(2) Is the product likely to be purchased with individual or family funds?

(3) Is the product so expensive that the purchase involves a trade-off in purchasing other products for the family?

(4) Are family members likely to disagree about the product?

(5) Is the product likely to be used by more than one family member? If so, are product modifications necessary to accommodate different persons?

(6) Which family members will influence the purchase and what media and messages should be used to appeal to each?

(7) Are particular stores preferred by various family members or families in the target market?

Forward-thinking companies can anticipate and take advantages of trends that are likely in the future.

Fig. 3.3: Family Decision-making

Q11. Define the culture and subculture.

Ans. Culture: To understand the influence of culture on consumer behaviour, we can define culture as the "sum total of learned beliefs, values, and customs that serve to direct the consumer behaviour of members of a particular society."

The 'belief' and 'value' components of our definition refer to the accumulated feelings and priorities that individuals have about "things" and possessions. More precisely, beliefs consist of the very large number of mental or verbal statements (i.e. "I believe...") that reflect a person's particular knowledge and assessment of something (another person, a store, a product, a brand). Values also are beliefs. Values differ from other beliefs, however, because they meet the following criteria: (1) They are relatively few in number; (2) they serve as a guide for culturally appropriate behaviour; (3) they are enduring or difficult to change; (4) they are not tied to specific objects or situations; and (5) they are widely accepted by the members of a society.

Therefore, in a broad sense, both values and beliefs are mental images that affect a wide range of specific attitudes that, in turn, influence the way a person is likely to respond in a specific situation. For example, the criteria a person uses to evaluate alternative brands in a product category (such as Samsung versus Panasonic HDTV sets), or his or her eventual preference for one of these brands over the other, are influenced by both a person's general values (perceptions as to what constitutes quality and the meaning of country of origin) and specific beliefs (particular perceptions about the quality of South Korean-made versus Japanese-made televisions).

In contrast to beliefs and values, customs are overt modes of behaviour that constitute culturally approved or acceptable ways of behaving in specific situations. Customs consist of everyday or routine behaviour. For example, a consumer's routine behaviour, such as adding a diet sweetener to coffee, putting ketchup on scrambled eggs, putting mustard on frankfurters, and having a pasta dish before rather than with the main course of a meal, are customs. Thus, whereas beliefs and values are guides for behaviour, customs are usual and acceptable ways of behaving.

Subculture: Not all segments of a given society, however, display the same behavior pattern. This is partly due to 'ethnicity' – the basic origins from which these segments emanate or different religious beliefs or even climatic and geographical considerations. It is therefore possible for a marketer to identify more homogeneous subgroups within the heterogeneous national culture. These subgroups are referred to as subcultures. The members of a specific subculture display customs, values and beliefs which are distinct enough to set them apart from the other segments in the same culture. However, in addition to the above different beliefs values and customs, they conform to the dominant values and behavioral patterns of the larger society to which they belong. To take an example, if we refer to the Indian society as the larger "Culture" segment, the various religious subgroups like Hindus, Muslims, Sikhs and Christians, represent the religious subcultures. They may possess different religious beliefs and customs, but are also similar in the sense that they all display common value system as Indians. In a multi racial society like America, there is an American way of life which typifies the American Culture, the various social groups like blacks, hirpanics and Asians display values and customs which are typical of them as subsegments. Each of these then represent a subculture. Subcultures therefore can be defined as a distinct cultural group that exists within a layer, complex society as an identifiable segment in terms of its beliefs customs and values.

Q12. How are cultural values relevant to a marketing practitioner?

Ans. Cultural values together influence consumer behavior in several ways such as methods of shopping, tastes and preferences. It is necessary, therefore, to understand a society's basic value structure before marketing to it. Different social classes may respond to cultural values in different ways. Consider the cultural value of achievement, for example. While all individuals may share the same ' cultural values, their methods of responding to them may differ greatly, depending on the sub-culture and social class.

Each culture has what is termed the *core values*. These are the dominant or basic cultural values. It is not necessary that the core values be exclusive to a particular culture. Several values are borrowed as people emigrate to societies.

While somewhat obvious to you, the important fact is that these values are pervasive and accepted as givens. For example, core values that have been cited may be any of the following:

(1) Progress, achievement and success: These values lead to progress for society

(2) Activity: Being and keeping active is widely accepted as a healthy and necessary part of life.

(3) Humanitarianism

(4) Individualism

(5) Efficiency, Practicality

Commonly held cultural values shape consumption choices to a large extent. Marketers Therefore,try to appeal to consumer values through advertising. These values influence both, product and brand choices. It has been found that ***terminal values*** such as comfort, security, pleasure, are influential in the choice of product class. ***Instrumental values*** such as broadmindedness become important in the brand choice decision.

Q13. How does subculture analysis help a marketing in the segmentation exercise?

Ans. Marketers have tended to look at subcultures as specific segments in terms of the differential mores of these subgroups result in consumption patterns and behavioral patterns specific to them. You have only to refer to the different customs followed by the various communities in India to understand how the marketer would like the consumption patterns at different religious festivals and performance of customary rites of these communities to identify distinct marketing opportunities. The different food habits of the geographical subcultures, for example, North and South India, represent possibilities for segmenting and targeting consumers for the food market.

Q14. Describe the types of subcultures.

Ans. Looking around us we can see that for multicultural societies, it is possible to identify several types of subcultures. We would briefly refer to the major types of subcultures here.

- **Racial or Nationality Subcultures:** Multiracial societies like America are today comprised of citizens who come from different nationalities or belong to different races. While they are subscribe to the wider concept of the core American values, each one of them display interesting differences for the marketer to be able to identify them as important, subculture segments. The broader American culture

Therefore,can be seen as consisting of the Afro-American subculture, the asian subculture the hispmic subculture to name some. These subcultures tend to vary in their values, aspiration and beliefs which get reflected in their consumption priorities, spend save patterns, purchase behaviour, use of credit, social mores and customs, etc. Marketers have found it useful to look at each of these subcultures as distinct market segments and tailor marketing plans to effectively reach them.

- **Religious Subcultures:** Most societies of the world today consist of people subscribing to different religions, which may differ in their beliefs, values and customs. We have referred to the Indian society earlier which is a good example of a multi-religion society. The religious subgroups may follow different custom, have important rites of passage (like birth, marriage, and death) performed in different ways and have different festivals. These in turn suggest items appropriate for consumption for the above activities which may not be common to all the members of the wider society. In addition, religion subcultures may suggest important "taboos" in consumption terms, certain foods are prohibited among the different groups, consumption of liquor or non-vegetarian foods may be specifically prohibited by some religious norms."
- **Geographical and Regional Subcultures:** Large countries, partly on account of geographical and climatic condition display geographical and regional differences which are distinct enough to enable marketer to envisage a country as consisting of different geographical or regional subcultures. One has only to look at our own country to clearly identify and appreciate the Gujarati, Tamil, Punjabi, Kasluniri, Bengali subculture identities with the Indian culture. Of special significance to the marketer are the various food preferences of these geographical regional subculture and the languages spoken in different regions. India today had 17 languages identified as official regional languages. These create unique challenges in terms of creating and delivering marketing communication. Geographical subcultures also result in different consumption patterns in clothing, housing patterns and food habits on account of climatic conditions. While cottons may be the most preferred fabric in North West India, silk predominates in South, Wollens have a very low priority in coastal regions as they are not required at all.
- **Age Subcultures:** You have already read about the stages in family life cycle and understand how consumption priorities change as the

age pattern of the family changes. Marketers have, on a more generic basis have been able to use age as a basis of identifying different subcultural identities as the youth market and the elderly market. The youth market (14-24) is important to marketers not only because it is a growing and lucrative segment but also because consumption preference found at this age are likely to continue for a long time. The youth market is distinctive enough in terms of its spending patterns, demographics, psycholography, profiles, etc. **Gender Subcultures:** It has been increasingly felt that as men and women vary in terms of dominant traits they posses, information search and processing norms they follow, gender may be indeed used as a subculture segmentation variable. While the traditional role identification of men as bread earners and women as homemakers are getting blurred, products can still be seen as being strongly associated or as exclusively developed for one sex or the other. Assignment also in terms of predominant decision making roles, tend to relate to gender subcultures. In behavioral terms, it has been found that consumers lend to assign a gender to products, in term of the perceived meaning of the product it may either be seen as a feminine or a masculine product. These are perceptions that need to be borne in mind by advertisers in addition to the gender of the target market. One gender subcultural segment that has been distinctively identified and used is the segment of the working woman.

Q15. Explain the personalities and motivational source of opinion leaders.

Ans. The personality theories that underpin personality tests and personality quizzes are surprisingly easy to understand at a basic level. The knowledge of personality theories and ideas helps to develop self-awareness and also to help others to achieve greater self-awareness and development too.

Developing understanding of personality typology, personality traits, thinking styles and learning styles theories is also a very useful way to improve your knowledge of motivation and behaviour of self and others, in the workplace and beyond.

Understanding personality types is helpful for appreciating that while people are different, everyone has a value, and special strengths and qualities, and that everyone should be treated with care and respect. The relevance of love and spirituality - especially at work - is easier to see and explain when we understand that differences in people are usually personality-based.

What Motivates Opinion Leaders?: Three reasons have been suggested as the forces motivating opinion leaders. One is that, they may use conversations as a dissonance reducing process for products they have bought. Or they may want to influence a friend or neighbour. Another reason can be self-involvement, when they may want to confirm their own judgement.

Can opinion leaders be reached through any specific media? Yes. Some studies indicate that opinion leaders possess a keener level of interest for particular product categories and, specific media, than opinion receivers in general. Opinion leaders are more exposed to the media. This is particularly true of media reflecting their areas of interest. Opinion leaders go to more movies and watch more television. They also read more magazines. There is more exposure relevant to their areas of interest. They also have greater readership of special and technical publications devoted to the product category. Such special interest magazines place them in a better position to make recommendations to relatives, friends and neighbours. It is not necessary, however, that opinion leaders have more exposure to the mass media in general.

People very rarely set out to cause upset - they just behave differently because they are different. Completing personality tests with no knowledge of the supporting theories can be a frustrating and misleading experience - especially if the results from personality testing are not properly explained, or worse still not given at all to the person being tested.

Q16. Discuss the opinion leadership process.

Ans. The process of opinion leadership has been described in simple terms as the two-step flow of communication. According to this, ideas flow from the media to opinion leaders and, from there to the general public. This two-step flow of communication portrays opinion leaders as direct receivers of information from impersonal marketing sources and, they therefore, serve as a vital link in the transmission of information.

The two-step flow theory has subsequently been modified into the more complex model of multi-step flow. This takes into account the fact that, social interaction between people serves as the principal means by which information is transmitted. In other words, the mass media alone, are not responsible.

According to the multi-step flow model, information is transmitted by the mass media to three distinct sets of people namely, the opinion leaders, the gate keepers and the opinion receivers or followers. Communications can be transmitted back and forth between these three groups.

As the multi-step flow model suggests, opinion leaders do not influence a passive group of followers.

This influence is, moreover, informal and interpersonal. In this process one party, the opinion leader usually passes on information and advice. The kind of product-related information that opinion leaders are likely to transmit are:

(1) How to use a specific product?

(2) Which of several brands is best?

(3) Which is the best place to shop?

Q17. Explain the relationship between Opinion Leadership and Product Specificity.

Ans. Opinion leadership is, however, product specific. Thus, an opinion receiver for one product category may become an opinion leader for another. However, opinion leadership product category may become an opinion leader for another. However, opinion leadership for related product categories does show a tendency to overlap. For example, people who are opinion leaders for small appliances may also be opinion leaders for large appliances.

Opinion leaders do not; however, seem to exert their influence across a range of unrelated product categories. This tends to happen because, since opinion leadership is a two-way process, an opinion leader who is knowledgeable about a particular product can very well become an opinion receiver for some other product.

Opinion leaders have been found to be a function of interest and personal expertise in a particular area. Opinion leaders tend to specialise in certain product categories about which they offer information and advice. Thus, for instance, you would find that, opinion leadership in fashion is not necessarily associated with opinion leadership in another area such as kitchen appliances. Again, opinion leaders for dental products are not necessarily influential in other areas.

Q18. Differentiate between the terms household and family.

Ans. Using the term household covers situations where the word family may not be appropriate - for example, if two people who are not married are living together, they certainly constitute a household, but one could argue about whether they constitute a family.

Family can also be difficult to define when families split up - for example, if the father leaves the mother and children, you could say he is still part of the family, but he is not part of the household.

The family is not just a social group. It is also an earning, consuming, decision-making unit, and it is of importance to marketers because of the influence that family members have on purchase and consumption decision. In this section we will consider the various family related factors that have an impact on consumer decision-making.

The family's influence comes from the fact that the bonds within the family are likely to be much more powerful and intimate than those in other small groups. Because of these bonds, the family has profound social, cultural, psychological and economic influence on consumers. Within the family, operating as the unit of analysis, a reciprocal influence operates on all decisions. There are three main sources of influence in the family decision process. These are the father, the mother and other family members.

Since a particular family may have several persons in the 'other family members' category, the decision process for a given family can be complex. Every family member brings his or her own motives, evaluations, beliefs and predispositions to the decision process. Every family member becomes part of the environment for the other family members and, influences, and is influenced by them. And the cognitions, behaviour and environments of the several persons become an important consideration for the marketer, as do the interactions of the members among themselves.

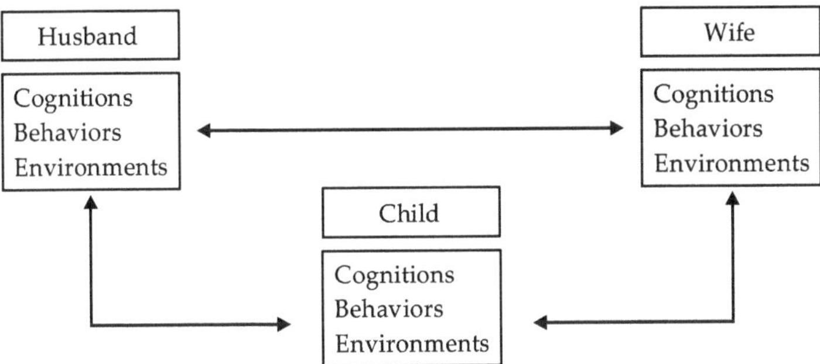

Fig. 3.4: The Reciprocal Influence of Family members

The terms for describing living arrangements are determined by the Bureau of the Census. Over time, these definitions change somewhat depending upon prevailing conditions.

A family is the term applied to a household that is composed of a number of people who are related either by "blood" or marriage.A non-family household is a number of people who live together but who are not otherwise related. For example, three male roommates who share an apartment while attending college is a household, but not a family. For example, if there is a family consisting of mother, father, two brothers, and one sister, and one of the brothers is away on a job or at college, only the four living in the same house are counted as a family household. The brother who lives someplace else will be counted as a single-person household if he lives alone, otherwise he'll be part of a non-family household.

Q19. Illustrate consumer socialisation.

Ans. It is an aspect of socialisation in which a person, in particular, a child acquires skills, knowledge, habits, and attitudes related to their behaviour in marketplace.

Factors Influencing Consumer Socialisation: There are several distinct factors that influence the consumer socialising process. These are:

(1) The Background/Environmental Factors: These include the environmental factors such as social and economic status, social class, age, sex, and religious affiliation of the consumer.

(2) The Socialising Agents: These include individuals who have direct influence on the consumer such as parents, sisters, brothers, peers, teachers and the media. The family is found to be important in teaching the rational aspects of consumption while TV viewing encourages consumption for emotional reasons.

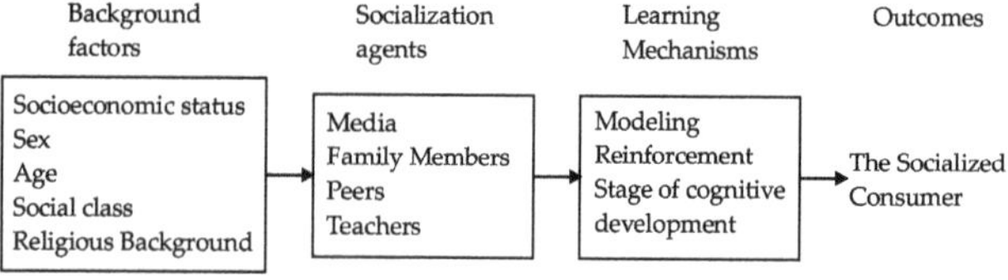

Fig. 3.5: A model of consumer Socialization

(3) The Learning Mechanism: Consumer socialisation occurs through two types of learning. One is the imitation of others by observing the actions of others in the family. What is learnt early in life has a lasting effect on most people. Brand loyalty is Thus, transmitted from parents to children and, favouured brands may persist for periods of anywhere up to twelve years or longer. The second type of learning is operant conditioning. This means that consumption behaviour that receives praise and is complimented likely to be repeated by a child while actions, that are ridiculed or, are less likely to have a negative outcome be repeated.

Consumer socialisation occurs in subtle ways that are not always obvious. There are four primary ways in which family influences can be transmitted to the individual within the family:

(i) **The parents act as models** for the child on numerous consumption occasions. The child learns through observation without the parents' conscious awareness or intention to teach.

(ii) **Parent-child discussions** about particular products or brands, why they are good for you, and why they are not.

(iii) **Child-child interactions.** These become an important socialising influence when more than one child is present.

(iv) **The child begins to handle** money as he or she becomes older. Thus, through gifts and allowances, the family provides opportunities for a child to become more experienced as a consumer.

Q20. Define the cultural values and changes.

Ans. The kind of learning characteristic of human children is "Imitative learning," which "means reproducing an instrumental act understood intentionally." Human infants begin to display some evidence of this form of learning between the ages of nine and twelve months, when infants fix their attention not only on an object, but on the gaze of an adult which enables them to use adults as points of reference and Thus, "act on objects in the way adults are acting on them." This dynamic is well documented and has also been termed "joint engagement" or "joint attention." Essential to this dynamic is the infant's growing capacity to recognise others as "intentional agents:" people "with the power to control their spontaneous behaviour" and who "have goals and make active choices among behavioural means for attaining those goals."

The development of skills in joint attention by the end of a human child's first year of life provides the basis for the development of imitative learning in the second year. In one study 14-month old children imitated an adult's over-complex method of turning on a light, even when they could have used an easier and more natural motion to the same effect. In another study, 16-month old children interacted with adults who alternated between a complex series of motions that appeared intentional and a comparable set of motions that appeared accidental; they imitated only those motions that appeared intentional. Another study of 18-month old children revealed that children imitate actions that adults intend, yet in some way fail, to perform. Tomasello emphasises that this kind of imitative learning "relies fundamentally on infants' tendency to identify with adults, and on their ability to distinguish in the actions of others the underlying goal and the different means that might be used to achieve it." He calls this kind of imitative learning "cultural learning because the child is not just learning about things from other persons, she is also learning things through them — in the sense that she must know something of the adult's perspective on a situation to learn the active use of this same intentional act. He concludes that the key feature of cultural learning is that it occurs only when an individual" understands others as intentional agents, like the self, who have a perspective on the world that can be followed into, directed and shared.

When the concept first emerged in eighteenth- and nineteenth-century

Europe, it connoted a process of cultivation or improvement, as in agriculture or horticulture. In the nineteenth century, it came to refer first to the betterment or refinement of the individual, especially through education, and then to the fulfillment of national aspirations or ideals. In the mid-nineteenth century, some scientists used the term "culture" to refer to a universal human capacity.

Culture can be defined as below mentioned process:

- A new pattern of behaviour is invented, or an existing one is modified.
- The innovator transmits this pattern to another.
- The form of the pattern is consistent within and across performers, perhaps even in terms of recognisable stylistic features.
- The one who acquires the pattern retains the ability to perform it long after having acquired it.
- The pattern spreads across social units in a population. These social units may be families, clans, troops, or bands.
- The pattern endures across generation.

❑❑❑

4

The Buying Process

Q1. How does the problem recognition stage vary between a low involvement and a high involvement purchase? How can the marketers benefit from these variations?

Or

Discuss the problem recognition process in case of consumer goods.

Or

Write a short note on Problem Recognition Stage in the Consumer Decision Process.

Ans. Customer behaviour study is based on consumer buying behaviour, with the customer playing the three distinct roles of user, payer, and buyer. Relationship marketing is an influential asset for customer behaviour analysis as it has a keen interest in the re-discovery of the true meaning of marketing through the re-affirmation of the importance of the customer or buyer. A greater importance is also placed on consumer retention, customer relationship management, personalisation, customisation, and one-to-one marketing.

Problem Recognition is the very first stage of the long process of consumer decision-making and is important for several reasons. Firstly, it provides an initial clue as to why a buyer buys what he or she intends to. Secondly, it gives a definite direction to his or her subsequent purchase behaviour stages like information search and evaluation of alternatives. Finally, it provides marketers with an immense scope for using their influence in how the buyers may or may not recognise their needs. Thus,a 'virtuous circle' exists between problem recognition by consumers and marketers stimuli or cues that prompt consumers to react in a desired manner. Given figure exemplifies this circular relationship.

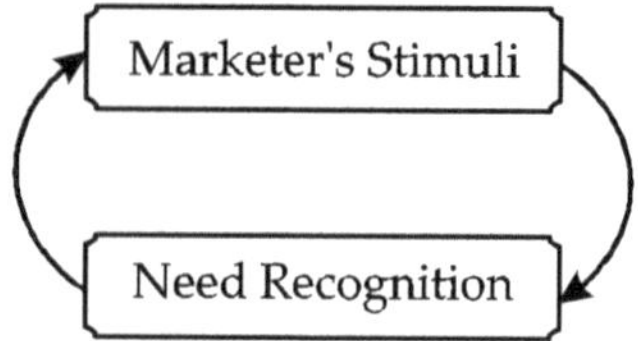

Fig. 4.1: Problem Recognition — A Consumer-Marketer Nexus

Even there is also a scope for classifying consumers on the basis of their different problem recognition styles. The first category of consumers are those who presume that they have a problem when their product fails to perform satisfactorily. For example, a wrist watch bought by a consumer no longer keeps accurate time. The second type of customers are those who recognise the need or problem not because the existing product has failed to perform but because of their desire of possessing something new. This partly explains why Titan watches found a ready market even though the HMT wrist watches more or less were quality performance products.

Need or problem recognition can be both simple and complex configurations, subject to associated conditions. Simple problem recognition refers to needs that occur frequently and can be dealt with almost automatically. For instance, while shopping with your friends in the market, you sighted a soft-drink stall and decided to buy a cold drink. This could also be to reduce the boredom of waiting out your friends to rejoin at a place.

Complex problem recognition however, is that state in which a problem recognition develops slowly but distinctly over a long time. At a certain time, the desired state of consumer mind is distinctly apart from the actual state. This causes him to recognise the need. For example, after several years of using a car, the car-owner begins to consider trading it in for a new one. The reason could be any ranging from mounting repair bills to the availability of several new models.

The existing consumer position reflects how a consumer feels presently about his consumption or non-consumption of a given product. The desired consumer situation refer to his expectations and anticipations from the, consumption or non-consumption of a given product and service. Most often, the perceived gap/discrepancy between these two stages fashions the needs of the consumer. Thus, as consumers grow up physically, financially and psychologically, there will be a perceived gap between their current and desired situations. A growing child will desire first a tricycle, then a bicycle and then, perhaps, a moped or motor cycle. Similarly, a housewife will plan her shopping once she notices a stock-out situation in her kitchen or in other household supplies.

At the current state of mind, marketers may 'induce' dissatisfaction in the consumers for the current stock of products and services. The marketers may also convince the buyers how obsolete the products have become. Mostly, this dissatisfaction is pointed towards `obsolete' functioning, style and technology. The efforts of markets in respect of existing or current state of consumption are however, quite limited. They are somewhat negative in nature too. Hence, most efforts are made by the marketers to condition the 'desired' state of mind of consumers.

Q2. Write down the threshold level in problem recognition.

Ans. Problem recognition represents the perceived gap between the existing and desired state of mind of consumers, which is influenced considerably by marketers' stimuli, However, it should be noted here that every 'gap' between these states of mind for a product or service will not result automatically in its 'need', The perceived gap must cross a threshold level if a need for the product were to become a felt need Thus,ignite the buying process.

The threshold level refers to "the minimum amount of tension, energy or intensity which is necessary for the feeling to occur".

Thus, marketing efforts are directed not only towards creating a gap between the current and desired states of mind of consumers but they are also towards increasing the tension level where need recognition is ensured. Examples of such marketing efforts include easy repayment or credit facilities for various durable and non-durable products offered by the manufacturers themselves or collaboration with others like a lease finance company or a bank. Many times, marketers increase the tension among consumer just by comparing consumers with whom that have bought their product. The tension increases leading to need recognition.

Q3. Why is information search behaviour so important to the marketers? Discuss the media available to marketers in helping external search.

Ans. The marketing implications of the search behaviour are broad ranging. For one thing, it makes marketers aware of how customers search for relevant information and for another, it helps them facilitate the search process in favouur of their marketing stimuli. Broadly, the marketers influence the search process through the areas of advertising, product and packaging policies and pricing.

Advertising poses a complex problem to marketers because consumers have a tendency of selective reception and perception. This adversely affects the marketers efforts in advertising and forces them to continuously monitor the effectiveness of advertising. With passage of time, audience-erosion occurs in the receptivity of advertisements. Further, interpretation of stimuli may convey to consumers a picture much different than what the markets had intended. Marketers may also vary the contents of products periodically and its packaging design. It not only averts the potential boredom among consumers but also conveys an image of moving with time and preference changes by the marketers. The introduction of words like 'new' 'improved' 'better' or 'power packed' are just the examples of this strategy followed by Indian marketers in recent times. Changes in packaging design and colour can further stimulate the consumers search process and push information process through the threshold level of attention.

In pricing, the marketers may convey a desired price quality perception among the buyers by effectively reviewing pricing permutations and combinations. Consumers may look at price-tags to acquire information about the quality variations and perceptions and to determine their own level of confidence in these matters.

Q4. Define the meaning of information processing and its marketing implications.

Ans. Information processing is a relatively recent addition to the lexicon of consumer behavior and therefore, a fair amount of unanimity exists in defining the term. Thus, it is described as "a series of activities by which stimuli are transformed into information, stored and used" It thus serves the purpose of linking an individual with groups, situations and with marketing influences.

Marketing Implications: A marketer can ignore the understanding of consumer information processing only at his own peril. The following facts merit special attention in terms of aiding consumer's information processing mechanisms:

(1) The design of the message (use of colours, contrast, structure, etc.).

(2) The concept of proximity (the context in which the message is being given. For instance an advertisement for a serious product appearing in the slot for a humorous programme, etc.).

(3) The concept of selective exposure (the consumer tendency to skip the commercials or leaving the place during the commercial break or zapping the ads on the VCR).

(4) Influence of values (conforming or violating the values like respect to elders, love to the younger ones, ridiculing the marital relationship, etc.).

(5) The distortion in the physical stimulus properties (poor transmission causing distortion in the message or the picture of the marketing message, or, poor printing or composition of the newspaper or the magazine carrying a message, etc.).

(6) The information over-load (the situation where too much information is placed before the consumer and he feels completely overwhelmed by the enormity of it).

Q5. Elabouuurate the process of attention. What is meant by creative packaging as a device to gain attention by the marketers?

Ans.

Attention is 'the degree to which consumers focus on stimuli within their range of expo-sure'. Because consumers are being exposed to so many advertising stimuli, marketers are becoming increasingly creative in their attempts to gain attention for their products. Dynamic packaging of information or stimulus is one way to gain this attention. For instance, a jam and jelly maker in India portrayed recently an adult enjoying these product but chatting and fretting like a baby. However, the classic advertisement of ONIDA TV is the best example of creative attention gaining exercise by the marketers. Thus, in sum, attention is to take note of something.

Fig. 4.2: Consumer's Attention

Underscoring the paramount need of being always ahead in the art of gaining consumer attention, some media and communication consulting firms have established elaborate procedures to measure the attention of consumer on several fronts. Thus, for gaining attention to packages, or enhancing package effectiveness, they recommend using such instruments as an angle meter, which measures package visibility as a shopper moves down the aisle and views the package from different angles. Similarly, data from eye-tracking tests, in which consumers' eye movements as they look at packages and ads are followed and measured, can result in subtle but powerful changes that influence their impact.

Q6. Differentiate between interpretation and yielding.

Ans. Interpretation: Interpretation is supposed to have occurred "when the consumer has placed the stimulus into any known or familiar categories in their mind and have assigned the meanings to them." In general terms, interpretation refers to understanding. The process of understanding is just not the function of how effectively the message has been structured. The entire process is affected by factors like cultural values of the social system and the prior expectations of the receivers. The meaning in information processing is always a 'learnt meaning', i.e. dependent upon what is already part of consumer's learning prior to this informational input. It is further facilitated by the marketers' effort to simplify the message and break the complexity in part that could be understood.

Yielding: The yielding of the intended meaning of the marketing communication refers to the process of "yielding or the tendency to accept new or varied information or meaning there from and absorbing it in the cognitive structure and long term memory". In simple words, it refers to the act of agreeing or disagreeing with the incoming stimulus of the marketer. Thus, for instance, the fact that whether we yield or not the message of the marketers to pay a higher price for the environment friendly products, is an indication of whether we accepted the stimulus or not.

Q7. Explain the theory of closure in gaining attention.

Ans. The principle of closure implies that consumers tend to perceive an incomplete picture as complete. That is, we tend to fill in the blanks based on our prior experience. This principle explains why most of us have no trouble reading a neon sign even if one or two of its letters are burned out or filling in the blanks in an incomplete message. The principle of closure is also at work when we hear only part of a jingle or theme. Utilisation of the principle of closure in marketing strategies encourages audience participation, which increases the chance that people will attend to the message.

Q8. Describe the imaginal processing.

Ans. It seems that information processing means word processing. This is incorrect and wholly inappropriate particularly today when images seem to be overtaking the words in communicating the messages. Availability of computer graphics, the tendency of the consumers to rush through the messages and the decidedly better effectiveness of the pictures or images to convey the message must force the marketers to understand imaginal processing as well.

Another important issue is the pictures that words too seem to create. This is dependent on the power of suggestions and inferences or innuendos created by words. Sometimes the style of writing may force the consumer to visualize the whole consumption experience. Three aspects deserve our attention in this context the first is the imagery vividness. It refers to the aspect of clarity of the mental image that the message creates. The second factor is the message control. It refers to the ability to self-generate mental images and manipulation as soon as the cue(s) are given by the marketer. The third factor is the imagery style that reflects the willingness on the part of the consumers to habitually engage in the imaginal processing as soon as the cues are given. The situation is involuntary.

The final issue here is the use of the 'allegories and metaphors' in information and how the consumers process these symbolic messages. The first is the processing of metaphors, which is essentially, is the use of simile. The other is the personification. which represents the abstract qualities as if they were person.

Q9. Discuss the consitutents of alternative evaluation.

Or

What are the types of information sought?

Or

Explain the components of Alternative Evaluation in buying decisions.

Ans. The alternative evaluation process is the interplay of these four factors, i.e. Product Attributes, Utility Function of Each Attribute Importance weights of Attributes, and set of Brand Beliefs. After having ascertained that the brands under consideration possesses all the desired attributes, consumers will identify how their satisfaction (utility) will vary in response to changing levels of performance in those attributes. Thus, the potential car buyer will decide how much will it mean to him in utility terms if brand "X" of car possesses 4/10 level of performance in fuel-efficiency, instead of, say, 6/10 level of style. The same could be argued in the case of the female lipstick buyer. The advantage of utility function is that by combining the performance levels of salient attributes, consumers can make up what is called an 'ideal' brand. As a result of information search, consumers will have found the following with reference to his product needs:

Product Attributes: During information search, consumers may identify several attributes of their needed products. For instance, a person intending to buy a family car may find styling, low maintenance cost, fuel efficiency and price as the attributes of the car. Similarly, a female buyer of lipstick may conclude after information search that range of shades, packaging, price and prestige factor are the desired attributes. The product attributes vary with consumers. Further, they are always determined by consumer needs.

Utility Function: Attribute so identified has a utility function. However, the utility may not be functional all the time. It could be emotional. For instance, the attribute of fuel economy in the car has an obvious functional utility as well as the feeling that a person is aware of the macro need of saving precious fuel.

Importance Weights of Attributes: All attributes identified by a consumer are not likely to be of equal importance to them or others. Different buyers of similar products differ in their perception. Thus, for instance, a middle class car buyer may discover during information search that fuel-economy is more important than styling, while the reverse may be thought so by a high income buyer.

Set of Brand Beliefs: During information search, consumers come to know about different claims and standings of the brands-more commonly known as brand-image, on its salient attributes. The brand image helps consumers in believing which brand is more likely to have a particular attribute. It should be noted here that these brand beliefs are based on consumer perception and may sometimes be at variance with reality.

Q10. What is meant by choice heuristics?

Or

Write down the choice-making rules for evaluation.

Ans. At the stage of choice rule, consumers after having recognised the need for a particular product and service and also having completed information search for relevant criteria, 'combine and integrate the information in such a way that facilitates choice making' for that product or service. Consumers make a variety of choices over time with reference to various products and brands. These are made on the basis of certain criteria known as *choice rules* or *heuristics*. Such heuristics allow consumers to make complex decisions reasonably and effectively.

Fig. 4.3: Choice Heuristics

In spite of the research evidence that for most purchases, consumers engage in a rather unsophisticated choice processes, particularly in the matters of low and medium involvement products, marketers need to know about the choice heuristics. In particular, they need to know as to what criteria are available to consumers; which among them may be used and why; and which marketers' actions can help influence and benefit from the process of applying choice rules in purchase situations.

The Benefits of Choice Heuristics: To consumers, the use of choice rules or rules of thumb offer many advantages. They, for instance:

- provide with guidance while making decisions;
- offer a short cut to a decision;
- allow them to integrate and arrange information in such a way that decisions may be made quickly and easily; and
- in consumer information processing help them better in facing complexities.

The Use of Choice Rules: Purchase decisions may be simple or complex. Three types of buying decision are normally there. The most complicated buying decision behaviour is known as Extended Problem Solving (EPS). It is seen mostly for high involvement products. The second type is the Limited Problem Solving (LPS). It is mid-range decision-making. The most common and routine process is called Routine Response Behaviour (RRB). The last one is most evident in respect of low involvement products.

The Choice Rules and the Multi-attribute Choice Models: Multi-attribute choice models explain how consumers combine their beliefs about product attributes to form their attitudes about various brand alternatives. These models assume that the brand which receives the best attitude will be chosen. They further assume that consumers will go through the standard Hierarchy of Effects sequence (Awareness - Interest - Desire - Action).

The Choice Rules and the Ideal Brand Model: This model prescribes that a consumer will compare actual brands to his ideal brand. The closer an actual brand comes to this ideal, the more it will be preferred. For instance, assume that the consumer does not rate the attribute of style in a product beyond a certain point. This may be because he has no particular fascination for it and it adds to his concern for upkeep. Let us further assume that the consumer also has a certain price in mind. Now whether the consumer will be satisfied or not with the available products will be determined by the following formula:

$$D_{jk} = W_{ik}[B_{ijk} - I_{ik}]\sum_{i=1}^{n}$$

where D_{jk} = consumer's dissatisfaction with brand K

I_{ik} = consumer's ideal level of attribute i

W_{ik} = importance weight assigned by consumer k to attribute i

B_{ij} = consumer k's belief as to the amount of attribute I offered by brand j

n = the number of important attributes in the selection of the given brand.

Q11. Explain some basic heuristics for the Limited Problem Solving (LPS) and Routine Response Behaviour (RRB) purchase situations.

Ans. At the end of the day, whatever may be the complexity or confusion in the mind of the customer, a decision is to be made. The following choice rules could come very handy to the consumers. It has been observed in most buying decisions, that most consumers try to 'satisfies' their purchase goals instead of maximising them. Often it becomes imperative in view of the complexities involved. Also, since majority of products engage only mild to low degree of purchase involvement, a complex treatment is not really required for buyers of these products.

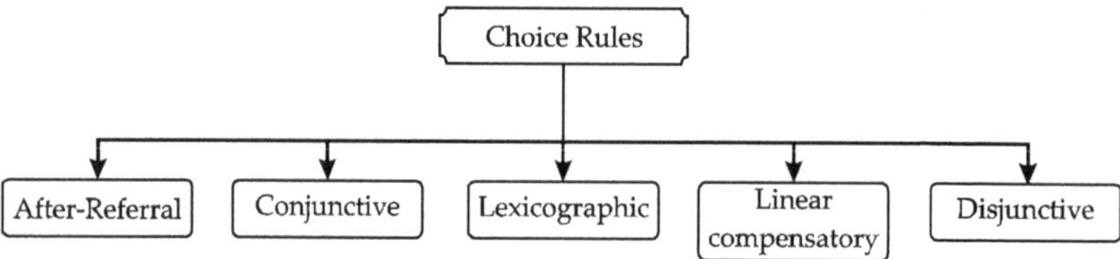

Fig. 4.4: Basic Choice Heuristics

The After-Referral Heuristic: In this choice rule is considered to be the simplest of all. Here the consumers obtain information from their earlier experiences stored in their own memory regarding the brand alternatives tried in the past. Thus, instead of evaluating brand attributes individually, a holistic approach is used by consumers based on their most positive feelings about a given product. In the case of RRB' and habitual purchases, this rule is most likely to be applied. Thus, for example, in the purchase evaluation of such daily consumption items as cigarettes, salt, tea, etc. consumers will elicit the brand alternative from their memory and past experiences in an order of their positive feelings for them. The brand that was purchased last and fulfilled most of its promise, is most likely to be chosen this time also.

The Conjunctive Heuristic: In a situation where many brand alternatives are available with distinct attributes, even though it is an LPS purchase situation, the conjunctive heuristic helps consumers in screening the brands. Over here, consumers set the minimum cut-offs on each attribute which every brand alternative under consideration must possess. Otherwise, the brand alternative is rejected. The conjunctive choice heuristic aids in screening brand alternatives, it weighs negative information more than the positive information in the evaluation.

The Lexicographic Heuristic: This choice rule is more positive in nature than the conjunctive heuristic. This heuristic aims, instead of rejecting the bad ones, at selecting the best brand alternatives out of the given alternatives. In order to apply this heuristic, buyers first rate the importance of attributes in the brands alternatives. Thereafter, the brand alternative are rated on these attributes. The brand alternative that scores the highest on the most important attribute is chosen, regardless of other attribute values. If all the brand alternatives score equally on this attribute, then their scores on the second most important attribute is considered and the highest scoring brand is chosen. The process goes on till the differential performance scores settle the superiority of a brand alternative over the rest.

Linear Compensatory Heuristic: In this rule, consumers permit the strength of a particular brand attribute to compensate for the weakness of another attribute(s). The choice criterion again is 'choose the best' because in the rule the effect of both positive and negative information is considered, which can balance, offset or compensate each other. Even though the chosen brand alternative is weaker on the attribute of low maintenance cost than others, the strength of other attributes has compensated for its weakness.

The Disjunctive Heuristic: The disjunctive heuristic, used quite infrequently, also sets the minimum cut-off points for every brand attribute. The difference, however, lies in the fact that this, heuristic stresses only the 'salient' brand attributes (on the basis of weights) and accepts a brand alternative if its performance exceeds the minimum cut-off performance on these dominant attributes.

Q12. Explain the purchase process and its importance.

Or

Identify the benefits or implications of the purchase stage to the marketer as well as to the consumer.

Ans. The purchase process marks the recognition of actual purchasing environment and its obvious effects on the process. All that marketers know about is supposed to happen in the mental framework of consumers. This is the stage where marketer can observe how mental evaluation is translated into purchase activity at the point of purchase. The importance of purchase process is further increased by following two reasons – one each from marketers and consumers perspective.

From marketers' perspective, purchase process is linked to marketing-mix. Thus, if customers purchase the evaluated item, it confirms effectiveness of the marketing mix employed by marketers vis-à-vis competitors. The non-selection on the other hand, will signal to marketers towards the need of a change in marketing mix, after a careful analysis of underlying reasons for brand rejection.

For customers, purchase action marks the end of their efforts for an optimum brand choice. Not only do they give up money in return for a product, but the choice of brand once made, also means that they must depend on it alone for the delivery of expected benefits and satisfaction, at least until next purchase occasion.

Q13. Discuss the determinants of situational influences.

Or

Write a short note on Buying Stage and Situational Influences.

Or

Write a short note on Situational Influences on Buying Process.

Ans. Situation, in general, is defined as "something outside the basic tendencies and characteristics of the individual but beyond the characteristics of the stimulus object to be acted upon". Thus, *physical surroundings* include noise, light, or temperature in the store. *Social surroundings* refer to the type of clientele patronising the store. *Task definitions* include motives for shopping and goals. *Temporal factors* comprise time-pressure and time of the day chosen for shopping. Finally *antecedent states* refer to cash and funds situation and the mood under which the purchase is completed.

Physical Surroundings: Research has now clearly highlighted the influence that physical surrounding have on consumer choice. Physical surroundings are the most readily visible features of a purchase situation because they include geographical and institutional location, decor, sounds, aromas, lighting, weather and visible configurations of merchandise or other material surroundings in the purchase process. These stimuli influence the choice process through sight, hearing, touch, smell, and taste of consumers. In order to exploit the physical surroundings effect to the maximum, marketers use the concept of 'atmospherics' by devising and controlling a right mix of physical surroundings during purchase process. Music and crowd management are two very popular elements of atmospherics at the point of purchase.

Social Surroundings: Social surroundings have significance in shaping up the choice behaviour. There are a variety of situations in which the presence of others may influence choice process. In a store, for instance, after having noticed the presence of high-society people, you may buy a premium item even though you had intended to buy only a low-price product. Further, it may also affect your resistance to the store or enhance product credibility if you find highly respected people or friends known for their good sense in buying. Furthermore, shopping is often a social experience in which, besides the buyer and seller, many other persuasions interact. They also affect the communication. Following are some general findings in this respect:

- while shopping with friends, a consumer is likely to make more unplanned purchases and visit more stores,
- selling to unaided buyers is easier than to those accompanied with advisers,
- compliance to group views is there even though the buyer knows that others are wrong with reference to a given product choice.

Task Definition: A host of motives initiate the purchase decision-making. The motives decide both the content and direction of a purchase process. These buying purposes are what we call as task definition in the present context. Task definition influences the purchase process in the following ways:

- The purpose of purchase may alter the purchase outcome.
- The use situation of the product will determine the task definition.

Thus marketers use task definition as a prominent feature of purchase. Occasion-based marketing opportunities have been explored by Indian marketers.

Temporal Factors: For any given purchase, temporal factors Or timing play a decision role. These timings may range from the allocated minutes of a day to shopping, and to even a season of the year perceived relevant to the purchase. Time can be considered both in absolute units of measurement and in comparative terms. Temporal factors affect the purchase in the following ways:

- Availability of time will decide the purchase strategy for a given product.
- Higher the amount of available time, greater will be the information search.
- Time, when accompanied with other variables (like, hunger or happiness) can produce a more visible effect.
- Time-compression, a device in which marketers use time effectiveness for maximum impact, can be used by marketers.

Research on time and consumer behavior has indicated that an 'after five', shopper spends considerably less time in purchasing than a 'regular time' customer does. Similarly, it has been found that greater the time-gap between two purchases, higher is the probability of extensive information search.

Antecedent States: Finally, among situational variables, moods and physical states, and thoughts too have a bearing on purchase situation. A famished consumer is more likely to finish his shopping quicker than a contented consumer, keeping other variables as same. Similarly, a consumer frustrated at not finding the desired product or response at the earlier outlets, may reveal a certain amount of negativism towards the subsequent outlets he may visit for no fault of theirs. Mood, on the whole, has been found to have a significant influence with reference to product or outlet chosen, or even the attention to various advertising messages.

Q14. Suggest some non-store buying routes for buying jewellary.

Ans. There are five best known routes of direct or non-store buying. These are:

- **The in-home buyer** places an order from the home through mail or telephone or even a catalogue. Though such route of buying is quite known to business-to-business marketing (a retailer placing an order with a wholesaler or to a distributor), its scope is highly limited in India to only known and tested customers. For individual consumers, the in-home order placement is merely to avoid an extra-trip for the known, familiar and standardized items only.
- **Tele-marketing**, mostly western in origin, comprises using pre-paid telephones (known as toll free numbers in the West) by customers for product enquiries or purchasing. Owing to limited facility of telephones and widespread complaints in their functioning, this route of non-store buying is again confined to select cities and customers in India.

- **The mail-order buying** is the buying and selling of goods to be shipped from the vendor through the mail to the purchaser. Information about to be purchased may be found in catalogs, advertisements, on the web, etc. and purchase orders transmitted to the vendor by mail, telephone, or internet connection.
- **Direct in-home sales** is quite prevalent in India; especially as a large number of women in semi-urban and rural areas like to stay in-home while males do the major shopping mostly alone. Also, at many places, market structure is not available for sundry household items. In many cases, housewives prefer this route as it provides them with an opportunity to have pleasure in bargaining, total attention of salesmen and a convenience in buying individually consumed female product items. This route may, however, decline in importance as the store-shopping habits and freedom increase in the rural and semi-urban areas.
- **Videotext or interactive video** is the pointer to the kind of shopping in future. In this method, buyer-seller interaction occurs through TV sets and computer terminals. The buyer, while sitting home, may type in his purchase information and requirements through the keyboard of his computer terminal or switch on the desired channel on his cable TV or videotext facility. Highly limited to only a few consumers in metropolitan and major towns, this route of non-store-buying in India is currently little known. It may However,in future grow into a familiar and fascinating route of non-store buying in many countries.

Q15. Explain the theories of post-purchase evaluation.

Or

Write a short note on Post-purchase Evaluation.

Ans. There are several theoretical explanations that relate consumers' product expectations with its performance. Following table attempts a brief account of four such theories and their marketing implications. Although these theories somewhat over simplify a complex relationship between product expectations and performance, they succeed in emphasising the importance of post-purchase evaluation. This is the stage of decision-making that ensures repeat purchase and favouurable word of mouth advertising. It also determines consumers attitudes not only towards the product purchased and other products manufactured by the company but towards the company itself.

Table 4.1: Explanations of Expectation-performance Disparity

Theory	Major Assumption	Marketing Implication
1. Assimilation Theory	Disparity minimized by adjusting perceived expectations with performance	Overstate product claims
2. Contrast Theory	Disparity 'magnified'	Reasonably understate product claims
3. Generalized Negative Theory	Disparity to nedonically negative state-a general negative feeling	Consistent claims with performance
4. Assimilation Contrast Theory	'Minor' disparities are minimized while 'major' disparities are 'magnified' further	State product claims slightly above the actual performance but within consumers' range of acceptance.

Formation of Satisfaction/Dissatisfaction: Every purchase inevitably results into either satisfaction or dissatisfaction. Satisfaction is the expected outcome. It signifies "a confirmation that performance of the chosen alternative is consistent with its prior beliefs and expectations." Dissatisfaction, on the other hand, signifies an absence of such confirmation with reference to the outcome.

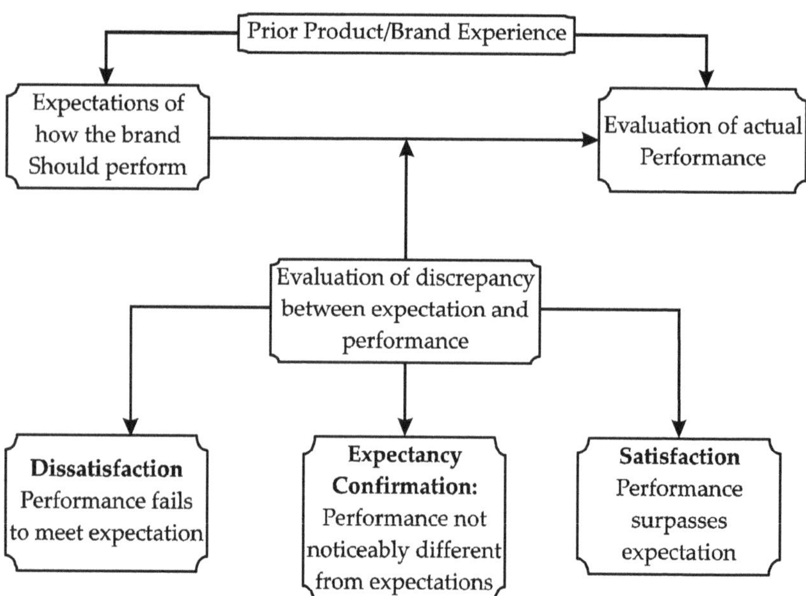

Fig. 4.5: Formation of Consumer Satisfaction/Dissatisfaction

Post-purchase behaviour has witnessed, in the recent past substantial research efforts. Some generalisations out of these researches are as follows:

- There is no all-accepted definition of consumer satisfaction or dissatisfaction.
- In many cases, while presence of a particular factor may cause dissatisfaction, the avoidance of it may not necessarily lead to satisfaction.
- Satisfaction/Dissatisfaction arises out of a cumulative effect of many factors. The individual impact of each is quite difficult to isolate.
- Although consumer dissatisfaction is all pervasive, it is unlikely to result always in complaint making. Authors have suggested that complaint behaviour is related to such factors as the level of dissatisfaction; the perceived gain from complaining, the personality of consumer; the general attitude towards complaining; the convenience in identifying the person to be complained against; the resources available to the consumer for complaining; and the previous experience with product and complaining clearly, handling satisfaction/ dissatisfaction is a logical process.

Q16. What are the marketers' response strategies?

Ans. A marketer has to design appropriate responses to post-purchase activities that will not only keep the consumer satisfied but also avoid the intervention of other parties in the matter. Following are the prominent responses that a marketer should consider in order to: build consumer satisfaction, maintain consumer satisfaction, avoid consumer dissatisfaction.

Monitor regularly the consumer reactions: A marketer should initiate and encourage a regular monitoring of consumer reactions towards itself, its product range and a particular brand. A continuous inflow of such monitoring data will develop into an information system and serve as early warning signals. Such monitoring is of particular significance where products are sold through non-store purchasing route.

Bring product quality under marketing responsibility: Though we hear a lot these days about improving product quality, nothing can substantially change until maintenance of product quality is brought under marketing responsibilities. Thus, quality control will upgrade itself from being an isolated function of production department to a joint mission of marketing and manufacturing departments.

Handle complaints quickly and responsibly: Marketers must go beyond the usual lip-service to handling of customer complaints. They should be taken up at the earliest opportunity and action notified to the complaint without delay. Even acknowledgement of the receipt of complaint contributes to reducing dissatisfaction.

Be a courteous and helpful host: Most of consumer dissatisfaction is attributable to poor service at the point of purchase. It may arise out of unhelpful or discourteous sales personnel, poor availability of product and inadequate service to customers. Marketers may note that even in standard products, considerable differentiation and competitive edge can be generated by being a courteous and 'helpful host to visiting customers.

State only realistic product claims: Factual promotion-executed with creativity, brings about lasting customer loyalty and goodwill.

Help consumer on product use: The manner in which the product is used can be crucial to customer satisfaction/dissatisfaction. It is in the interest of marketers themselves to help consumer in proper use of the product — especially those which may fail if wrongly opened or used blindly. Adequate instructions or information could be given to reduce potential consumer dissatisfaction.

Sell 'solution' instead of product: Nobody buys a product what consumer buy is 'solution' through products. Thus, promotional attempts should focus on the solution or performance of product rather than the product. This will signify the desire of marketers to provide satisfaction to customers.

Assure even after the purchase is over: Marketers must assure the buyers, even after the purchase is concluded of their commitment to customers' satisfaction. A thank-you letter or a visit to customers enquiring about their post-purchase feelings can go a long way in building a healthy and satisfying relationship for both customers and marketers.

Q17. What are the consumer buying process which faces the problem?

Ans. The consumer buying process is the series of steps consumers typically go through in making a purchase decision. Often the whole process will only take seconds or a few minutes, while other times it may take years. Regardless of how long it takes, consumers generally go through six steps when making a purchase decision:

- problem or need recognition
- search
- alternative evaluation
- purchase decision and action
- post-purchase evaluation

Problem or need recognition initiates the buying process. Dissatisfaction with current products, running out of supply of an item, or a changed financial status can stimulate consumer needs. Most consumers are creatures of habit and will repurchase the product they always use. This helps firms who are the established leaders in their markets but creates a barrier for new competitors. New competitors look for dissatisfied customers; those who are new to an area; and those who, through inheritance, divorce, or other situations have significantly changed their purchasing power.

In the search stage, consumers identify different products that will solve their problem. For everyday purchases like milk or bread, consumers usually quickly determine alternative sources of products to meet their needs. For high-involvement purchases like homes or automobiles, the search process will take longer and probably include searching for objective sources of information. Many consumers will only consider a few possible choices when searching for products to solve their problem. Marketers refer to the choices considered as the "evoked set." Firms that have severely disappointed consumers in the past or who are new to the market often have difficulty even being considered by consumers. n the alternative-evaluation stage, consumers consider and weigh the choices available. Again, with everyday-type purchases this stage can take seconds, while for a specialty item it may take months. Marketers respond to the alternative- evaluation stage by providing and promoting features they hope will influence consumers' evaluation of their products.

There can be considerable variation in the evaluation stage. One marketer found that it took him half the time it took his wife to do the family grocery shopping. Going to the supermarket together, he found out why. His wife read the ingredient labels, while he just purchased what was on the shopping list.

The purchase decision and action is, as the term suggests, the determination of which product will best satisfy one's need and the action of making the actual deal. Salespeople refer to this stage as the "closing." For everyday purchases, the goal is to make the purchase as quickly and effortlessly as possible. For complex decisions like a real estate closing, the purchase process can take weeks.

Post-purchase evaluation addresses the questions "Did I make the right decision?" and "Did I get a good deal?" Marketers refer to this anxiety as cognitive dissonance. Good marketers, recognising that word-of-mouth is almost always the best form of promotion and that new customers are almost always more difficult and expensive to find than maintaining existing customers, try to reduce consumers' cognitive dissonance. Realtors will offer buyer's insurance, protecting the purchaser against unforeseen problems. Service providers like dentists and doctors will often call clients to see how they are doing after a procedure. Thank-you notes convey appreciation and also remind consumers about their purchase process.

Q18. Define the various types of informat ion search.

Ans. There are many different types of information resources available.

Internet: Internet is tertiary sources information. Databases allow you to search across a range of journal articles from different journals.

Newspapers: Newspapers are primary sources of information. They are an excellent source when looking for current and up-to-date information. UCD Library provides access to both print and electronic versions of daily newspapers.

Websites: Websites are useful sources of current information and for an overview on a topic. Check our evaluating websites page to ensure the information you find is reliable. For a selection of reliable websites in your subject area, have a look at the relevant subject portal.

Search Engines: Search engines enable you to find information on the Internet. There are different types of search engines: meta search engines - that allow you to search several search engines at once, scholarly search engines - which search for academic information and normal search engines such as google.

(1) Sales personnel have a major role to play as a source of information for consumer durables like appliances, furniture, electronics and clothing etc., and in almost all industrial products. Being both expensive and uncertain in its effectiveness, this source of information is provided with immense care and caution by the marketers.

(2) Package information is used mainly to inform customers on the product ingredients and the mode of using it. However, the markets may use packaging colour and design to convey a favouurable brand personality.

(3) Advertising is the first major source of information. This has remained so in spite of the risks of overexposure and cluttering of advertising messages. The receptivity to advertisement pertaining to desired product category, goes up considerably once the customer has recognised his need problem for the product/service. Though varying in importance from case to case, advertising has been reported to have provided 35 to 50% of the information sought by the consumers in different purchase considerations.

(4) In-store material include, display-prices, brochures, danglers, technical report summaries. The material is useful for both soft-item purchases and the complex ones. Information on availability of dealers and distribution support and service is given either exclusively or as a part of advertisement. 'Yellow Pages' directory introduced in this country recently in metropolitan towns may emerge in near future a veritable source of information in this regard.

Finally samples and demonstrations are one of the most effective source of information to consumers. Besides being custom-built, the product demonstrations have now been standardized and used on a mass-media like television. Use of samples provides a risk-free source of information and may create a favouurable impact for marketers.

Q19. Give the reason to which the slow acceptance of direct marketing in India can be attribute.

Or

Define the anatomy of non-store buying.

Ans. "Direct (response) marketing is the total of activities by which products and services are offered to market segment in one or more media for information purposes, or to solicit a direct response from a present or prospective customer or contributor by mail, telephone or other access."

The non-store marketing owes its prominence to a variety of reasons. These reasons are:

- Greater importance to comfort in consumer life style
- Higher discretionary incomes
- Demand for convenience in shopping
- Option of credit facilities through credit or charge cards
- In-store crowd and long queues in delivery and payment
- Under-informed and little-trained store personnel
- Pressure for spot decision under stress of store personnel

The non-store buying option has become stronger not because of the sudden fad or fascination on the part of marketers or consumers. The economic environment also plays an important role in it. The development of non-store buying in a country is dependent upon several economic and social factors some of these are as follows:

- general economic development
- availability of logistics and infrastructure
- nature of product
- consumer awareness
- freedom enjoyed by marketing forces
- desire of marketers to reach new and uncovered market segments

However, we find varying degrees of direct marketing practiced in different countries. Be that as it may, direct marketing and its interaction with consumer buying process is of special significance but largely undeveloped because direct marketing itself is growing only recently. In India, for instance, we have the well-known examples of Bull worker, Readers' Digest who have successfully served their target segments through direct marketing.

❑❑❑

Feedback is the breakfast of Champions.

Ken Blanchard

Be the first one to report any mistake in Gullybaba Books.

You can Help other students.
"Inform any error or mistake in this book."

We and Universe will reward you for Your Kind act.

Email at : feedback@gullybaba.com
or
WhatsApp on 9350849407

5

Modelling Buyer Behaviour

Q1. Describe the various models which depict the consumers and their decision-making processes.

Ans. A variety of the early, traditional models, each explaining the behavior of the consumer from its own perspective and indeed taking a differential view of the consumers, exists. It is interesting to look at some of these early models to enhance our understanding of how the views of what makes a consumer 'tick' have changed over time and how each different input from related fields has furthered the available knowledge in this field.

Economic Models: The economic theory has given alternative views of the consumer from the view point of its sub-disciplines, i.e. micro-economic and macro economics.

Micro Economic Models: The micro economic approach was based on the way an 'average' consumer allocates his resources and then develops generalization about aggregates of such average consumers in the economy. The focus was on the act of purchase in terms of what customer bought and how much would be purchased. The inter play of needs and motivation, the prioritization of these preferences was not considered in developing the actual models.

Macro Economic Perspective: Macro economics, the field focused on aggregate flows in the economy, their direction and change over time, tries to draw generalizations about the behavior of consumers, who by their decisions, influence these flows. Two inputs from the Macro economic field are important for our understanding of consumer behavior. These are the *relative income hypothesis* and the *permanent income hypothesis*.

The Gestalt Model: This model lays special empahsis on man and his environment and on, the basis of controlled experiment, was able to give quite conclusive proof that individuals perceive and interpret the stimuli confronting them in relation to the organisation of their own individual experiences. The term 'gestalt' means form a configuration and the gestalt theory dealt specifically with the physical perception of stimuli.

Enlarging upon and modifying the gestalt approach, Lewing postulated that man lives in complex psychological field composed of many influences. If a realistic theory of motivation is to be formed, he said, all these influences must be realised and comprehended. By his contention, human activity is basically goal directed and individual behaviour of any sort is directed towards a stable organisation of- his psychological field, through attempts to reduce tension, reconcile conflicts and make sense out of the world in which he lives. This model, as noted earlier, was a step forward in the study of perception and interpretation of individual stimuli and may have implications for the marketer in planning his marketing strategy and particularly, brand strategy.

Sociological Model: The sociological model postulates that man's needs and behaviour are largely dependent upon and shaped by the social groups and forces. People tend to take the cue for their needs and wants, and how to fulfill them, from culture, subcultures, social class, reference groups, and family.

The social theorist Thorstien Veblen (19th century) suggested that "individuals are members of various social groups and they tend, under normal circumstances, to conform to largely unwritten but nevertheless powerful behavioural standards or norms of these social groups". Sometimes they emulate the behavour norms of the higher status groups to which, they aspire to belong. In subsequent years several social researchers confirmed this and reiterated that the purchase by individuals of various kinds of goods and services is likely to be strongly influenced by group norms of the group to which they belong or aspire to belong. The major source of influence on individual behaviour are the family, the culture and the subcultures that surround the individual, the reference group to which he belongs or aspires to belong and social class.

Q2. What do you mean by the theory of cognitive dissonance.

Or

Discuss the concept of Cognitive Dissonance and its implication for marketing discipline.

Ans. The cognitive theory or more pertinent to the understanding of buyer behaviour, the theory of cognitive dissonance has provided highly useful and rational explanation for the buyer behaviour.

Leon Festinger, the propounder of the theory of cognitive dissonance hypothesised that:

(1) The existence of dissonance (a state of imbalance in the cognitive structure) is psychologically uncomfortable and will lead the person to reduce

dissonance and achieve consonance (i.e. balance).

(2) Whenever dissonance exists, the person, in addition to trying to reduce it will also actively try to avoid situations and information which add to dissonance.

Consider the implication of such a process for the purchase and post-purchase behaviour of individuals. An individual strives towards equilibrium in his cognitive structure (set of beliefs and disposition about people, products, events etc.) and will strive to reduce tension in order to maintain this balance and render life pleasant. A disharmony (dissonance) may result from purchasing a product; after using it or receiving adverse reports about the product, especially if the product is an expensive one. "The magnitude of the post-purchase decision is an increasing function of the general importance of the decision and of the relative attractiveness of the unchosen alternatives".

Applied to day-to-day marketing situations, the theory interprets buying behaviour as follows — when several alternatives confront the buyer in his choice decision, he is likely to experience some anxiety, which becomes more insistent once a commitment to purchase one of them has been made. As advertisements and word of mouth information highlighting the qualities of the rejected alternatives are perceived and received, he may experience some doubts about the rationality of his decision. The product itself may not live up to his expectation and this adding to the already existing anxiety will give rise to what is called post-purchase dissonance.

According to Festinger, the buyer in this situation will try to reassure himself by seeking information to support his choice; and also by avoiding sources of information which would reduce his buying confidence. He may, in addition, collect information which projects the rejected alternatives disadvantageously. Being selective in his perception, therefore, the buyer may select the information supporting or favouurable to his choice and avoid or distort unpleasant information.

Q3. Discuss the Howard-Sheth model.

Ans. Efforts to analyse and understand behaviour of consumers have been on ever, since documented material on marketing activities has been available. In a major effort to integrate the available knowledge from 'the various fields, that impinge upon consumer decision processes, Howard and Sheth model, created a comprehensive body of conceptual knowledge link up most of the related concepts in buyer behaviour.

HOWARDSHETH MODEL - A BACKGROUND: Utilising the learning theory thoroughly and systematically, John Howard came out with the first truly integrative model of buyer behaviour in 1963. He was the first to introduce the difference between problem solving behaviour (similar to rational behaviour of the economic theory), limited problem solving and automatic response behaviour. A more meaningful elabouuuration was provided in the publication of "The Theory of Buyer Behaviour" in 1969 by Howard and Sheth. More variables impinging upon the behaviour of the consumer were included and the connection between them was clarified with noteworthy precision, making this model an important landmark in the development of the theory of buyer behaviour. A simplified version and description of the model is furnished below.

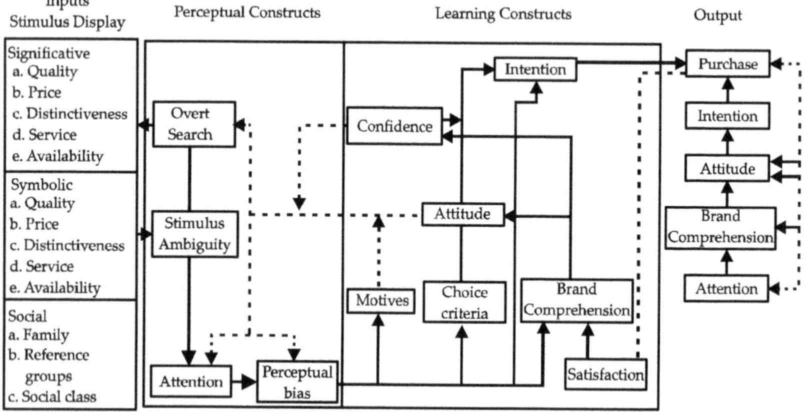

Fig. 5.1: Simplified Description of the Howard/Sheth Model

The model is essentially an attempt to explain brand choice behaviour over time and Therefore,specially pertinent to our field. Focussing on repeat buying, the model relies on four major components — stimulus inputs, hypothetical constructs, response outputs and exogenous variables.

Q4.What are perceptual constructs and learning constructs?

Or

Briefly describe the hypothetical construct.

Ans. The hypothetical constructs have been classified in two — the *perceptual constructs* and the *learning constructs*. The former deal with the way the individual perceives and responds to the information from the input variables. All the information that is received may not merit 'attention' and the intake is subject to perceived uncertainty and lack of meaningfulness of information received (stimulus ambiguity). This ambiguity may lead to an overt search for information about the product. Finally, the information that is received, may be, according to the buyer's own frame of reference and pre-disposition, distorted (perceptual bias). The learning constructs deal with the stages from the buyer motives to his satisfaction in a buying situation. The purchase intention is an outcome of the interplay of buyer motives, choice criteria, brand comprehension, resultant brand attitude and the confidence associated with the purchase decision.

The motives are representative of the goals that the buyer seeks to achieve in the buying exercise; these may originate from the basis of learned needs. Impinging upon the buyer intention are also the attitudes about the existing brand alternatives in the buyer's evoked set, which result in the arrangement of an order of preference, regarding these brands. Brand comprehension "the knowledge about the existence and characteristics of those brands which form the evoked set"; and the degree of confidence that the buyer has about the brand comprehension, choice criteria and buying intentions, converge upon the intention to buy. As a feedback component of learning, the model includes another learning construct-satisfaction which refers to the post-purchase evaluation and resultant reinforcing of brand comprehension, attitudes, etc.

The output variables consist of a set of possible hierarchical responses from attention to purchase. The purchase act is the actual, overt act of buying and is the sequential result of the attention (buyer's total response to information intake), the brand comprehension (a statement of buyer knowledge in the product class), brand attitude (referring to the evaluation of satisfying potential of the brand) and the buyer intention (a verbal statement made in the light of the above externalising factors that the preferred brand will be bought the next time the buying is necessitated).

Q5. How does the consumer's brand choice behaviour vary under EPS, LPS and RRB condition?

Ans. Since by the process outlined about the buyer tends to simplify his decision making behaviour; the phenomenon has been termed the 'psychology of simplification' by Howard and Sheth. The stages through which the routinisation is approached have already been outlined. The authors of the model taking the problem solving approach have designated these stages as:

(1) Extensive problem solving (EPS) behaviour.

(2) Limited problem solving (LPS) behaviour.

(3) Routinised response behaviour (RRB).

Extensive problem solving behaviour, corresponds to the first stage of repetitive decision-making where the buyer has not yet developed strongly predispositions towards any of the brands that are being considered as alternatives, nor does he have any well defined criteria at this stage. This stage is followed by the limited. Problem solving stage where because of learned experience about the brands, the choice criteria have a clear definition and organisation, but the buyer is still undecided about the actual choice among the alternatives. He has a moderately favouurable disposition towards some brands that fall in his latitude of acceptance (which is quite large at this stage) though this clear preference towards any brand has not yet crystallised. As repetitive choice decision continue to take place, limited problem solving matures to the routinised response behaviour.

Psychologists have used parallel terms to describe analogous stages corresponding to **EPS**, **LPS**, and **RRB**. The stages and their sequence are practically the same, the terminology used embraces the psychological aspect. According to them, when the buyer is in the initial stages of brand choice decision process, in the absence of any predisposition about any of the brands in his evoked set he is still in the stage of concept formation of the brand. On the basis of brand comprehensions active information sought and learning through use, he formulates the concept of the brand. In the corresponding LPS stage he has already attained the concept but is in the concept testing stage through which after testing the brands in use he has definite leanings towards one particular brand. In the subsequent purchases he utilises this concept (stage of concept utilisation) by making the choice decision accordingly in favouur of the preferred brand and minimising the number of alternatives considered because they do not match his concept.

Q6. Classify the current modeling efforts.

Ans. Fuelled by the experience of Howard-Sheth model and other parallel researchers, many more attempts have taken place to understand and ultimately model Consumer Behaviour. These attempts can be classified into different categories according to following main criteria:

(1) Modelling Objectives: The objectives of modelling have mainly confined to the following:

(i) Description of Buying Behaviour: Models with this objective focus upon the various constructs which play key roles in the buying process and behaviour. These constructs are highlighted through their locations in the schematic diagrams representing overall consumer behaviour. These models are like snapshots of the consumer behaviour. Thus, they are strong in representing the values that different variables of the model take. But, they are weak in explaining causality. One of the major use of such models is to communicate marketers visualisation of his consumers to his audiences. Models prepared with this objective are also found to be convenient starting points for building more complex and higher objective models. Various market definition or consumer profile surveys provide the data sources for achieving these objectives. Through such surveys the demographic, socio-economic, psychographic and other buying stages related data can be provided. These data can portray the consumers in terms of their key dimensions as well as on overall basis.

(ii) Describing the Consumer Processes: This objective focusses upon the processes which take place in influencing the consumer behaviour rather than the state of consumers. The objectives take the marketer one step closer to the causality models. They also help in linking various constructs and provide directions to these linkages within the models of consumer behavior. Whenever these linkages are quantified the marketer gets even stronger handles to design the input mix for achieving the resultant consumer states.

(iii) Predictability and Control of Consumer Behaviour: This is the ultimate objective of consumer behaviour modelling. It presupposes the data to describe the states of consumer behaviour as well as the relationships among them. Understandably, it is the hardest to achieve. For one reason, the knowledge base for achieving this objective depends upon the entire knowledge base in. marketing and rest of other disciplines connected with the prediction of human behaviour.

(2) Support of Basic Disciplines: The current model developments in the consumer behavior can also be seen through the utilization of the basic academic disciplines on which such models are mainly built. Economics, which gave the earliest conceptualization of consumer behavior, assumed consumer to be a rational economic entity. His choices were the focus of attention in economics at micro as well as macro levels. The restrictive assumptions made in the discipline and the multitude of human factors encountered in the practice of marketing reduces the utility of this discipline somewhat in modeling consumer behavior. Psychology, with its focus on the why of human behavior, has also contributed significantly to the knowledge and modeling attempts of consumer behavior. Almost every consumer behavior model uses; some psychological constructs. The understanding of these constructs and their relationships with other constructs are often borrowed from the mother discipline of psychology. The main problem with the psychological constructs had mainly been in the areas of their operationalizability in the context of marketing, weaker relationships encountered and exclusion of non-psychological variables. Sociology similarly has also been used significantly in understanding the group phenomena of consumers (such as market segmentation) and different social processes among consumers (such as diffusion of innovations).

(3) Support of Analytic Techniques: Consumer behavior models invariably deal with a multiplicity of variables. For coping with this situation; current consumer behavior models are using diverse analytical techniques. Most of these techniques were available in the literatures of mathematics, statistics and operations research. But, with the easy availability of sophisticated computing power, these techniques have started playing much greater roles recently. Thus, for example, stepwise regression analysis, correspondence analyses are very often used for identifying the salient variables and their relationships out of the observed data: Factor analysis and multidimensional scaling techniques are used for reducing data and drawing the essence from a large set of data. Very often consumers evaluation of different attributes and their relative trade-offs are important. Conjoint analysis has come as a handy tool for such purposes.

(4) Basic Unit of Consumer Behavior Models: Earlier consumer behavior models centred around the behavior of individual consumers. In fact, they further concentrated upon fast moving consumer nondurable products. This was, perhaps, easier as such models did not require considerations of interactions among different individuals involved in the purchase of same item. But, with the greater share of families, institutions and industries in the total purchase of products, these social units can no longer be ignored. Therefore, more and more models are surfacing whose units of decision-making are larger than individuals. Out of these, the most common units of decision-making are industries, distribution channel members and families.

Q7. Describe the Nicosia's model of consumer decision process.

Ans. This model elabouuurates the decision-making steps that the consumers adopt before buying goods or services. It is written in the format of a detailed computer flow chart. For ease of understanding the model can be simplified by grouping together its various elements into fields and subfields. Various components of the model are connected through direct as well as feedback loops. Thus, the marketing organisation affects the target customers. The customers, in turn, through the effects of marketers action affect the next decisions of the marketer himself. This process goes on. The main fields and subfields of the model are as following:

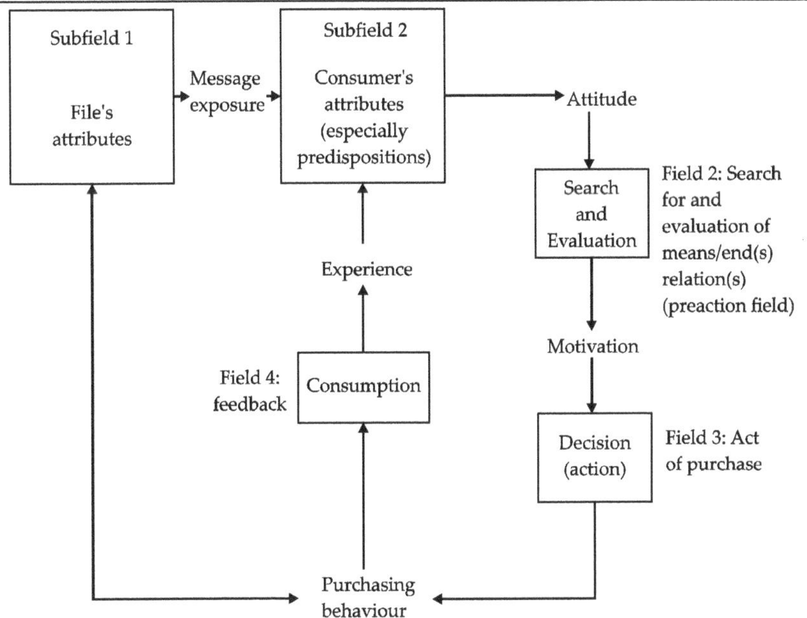

Fig. 5.2: Abridged Version of Nicosia Model of Consumer Decision Process

(1) Marketer's communication affecting consumers attitude: Here the marketing communications include not only mass media and personal communications but products, price and even distribution aspects, too. The exposure of these attributes affect consumer's attitudes as well as perceptions. These effects on consumers depend upon his personal characteristics (like values, personality, and cumulative experiences). After processing the inputs from marketer, the consumer forms his attitudes as the inputs for the next field.

(2) Consumer's search and evaluation: This step occurs before consumer becomes motivated to purchase the product. He seeks more information and evaluates the relative merits of competing products' attributes. The criteria for evaluation do also evolve with consumers past experiences and the marketer's inputs in the form of marketing mix.

(3) Purchase action: This is the field 3 of the Nicosia model. Here, after getting motivated to buy the brand, the customer actually shops for the product. The choice of actual retailer does also take place here.

(4) Consumption experience and feedback: After purchasing the product, the experience with its consumption can affect the consumers in many ways. The negative experience may block his future purchase and lower his attitude and evaluations of the product. The positive experience may motivate him further to be loyal to the product. In any case, the field provides significant feedback to the marketer. With this feedback, the marketer can suitable modify the next cycle's marketing inputs.

Nicosia's model may appear to be simple and obvious at the first glance. But its value lies in the integration of the body of knowledge in the area of consumer behaviour existing till its time of formulation. It does also provide insights about how the non-action kind of variables present in the environment and related to the consumers trigger actions at the consumers end.

Q8. Briefly describe the scanner and interrupt mechanisms in the Bettman model.

Ans. The Bettinan's consumer behaviour model focusses entirely on the information processing. The research attempts to validate it are also focussing upon the information handling by consumers. Consumers are encouraged to share the protocol that they mentally go through, while taking decisions. These methods are rich in providing consumer insights but difficult to administer practically. This model is also built around several flowcharts. These flowcharts describe the components and interconnections among themselves that are involved in the decision process. The main components of the model are the following:

(1) Processing Capacity: Each individual has a limited capacity to process information. This capacity can vary across individuals to some extent. But, its limits across all individuals are severally restrictive. Consumers try to by pass these limits by ignoring certain information, priortising information in use or using rules of thumb. Knowledge of the processing capacities of individual consumers and the ways they utilise these capacities provide invaluable insights to marketers.

(2) Motivation: Motivation provides the intensity and direction for the choice process to the consumer in this model. This acts as the superiding component and controls the continuation and suspension of various processes in the model like attention and scanning, etc. It also acts as the engine to convert the non-action or passive inputs to the customers into action outputs or overt behaviour of the consumer.

(3) Attention and Perceptual Encoding: This model divides attention into voluntary and involuntary attention. The voluntary attention is the conscious attention seeking to achieve the hierarchy of goals as set by the consumer for himself. The involuntary attention is triggered when the consumers have to resolve between the conflicting information received for processing or the short-term attention provided before deciding whether to process information through voluntary attention.

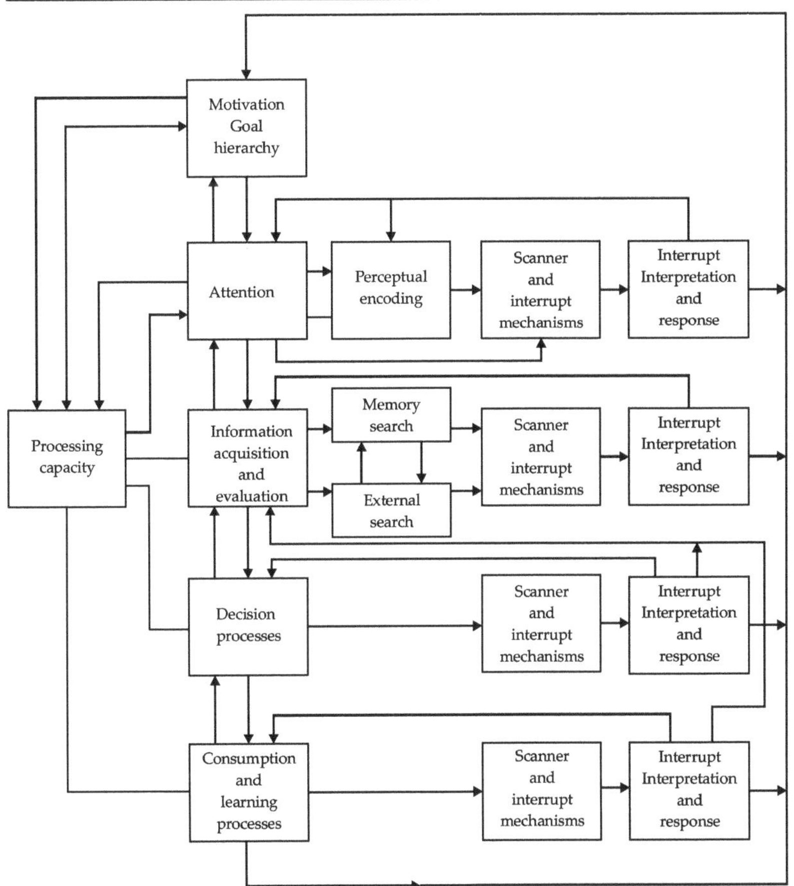

Fig. 5.3: The Bettman's Information Processing Model of Consumer Choice

(4) Information Acquisition and Evaluation: Within the scope of heuristics, the consumer also decides about the nature and amount of information that would be necessary and sufficient for decision-making. If the available information is found to be insufficient but necessary, he goes for acquiring further information through external search.

(5) Memory: Consumer memory comprises of short-term memory and long-term memory. In the short-term memory the acquired information is stored for less than two minutes. The consumer evaluates the impinging stimuli and decides whether the information is worth transferring to long-term memory or may be forgotten. If it goes to long-term memory, it is stored forever. Memory is the resource for the internal search for information. Only when it is found to be insufficient the external search is carried on.

(6) Decision Process: The ultimate decision of the brand is preceded by various sub-decisions about various aspects using rules of thumb or other methods of decision-making. These decision processes work on the acquired and evaluated information as well as the perceptions of the consumer. The situational factors (like time pressure, moods and company of other individuals, etc.)

(7) Consumption and Learning Processes: The experience gained through the consumption of products as well as the process of decision-making are stored by the consumers. These learnings affect not only the memory for the next cycle of decision-making but also affects the future heuristics for consumer decision making.

(8) Scanner and Interrupt Mechanisms: These are like the information switches of the consumers. Whenever the consumer decides that he does not have sufficient information for decision-making internally, he scans the environment for acquiring the necessary information. On the other hand, whenever he finds that he has sufficient information or acquiring more information is not worth the decision at stake, he shall interrupt the information search process.

Q9. Explain the meaning of exogenous variables & working relationship.

Ans. Mathematical model also known as Exogenous Variables.It can take forms, including but not limited to dynamical systems, statistical models, differential equations, or game theoretic models. These and other types of models can overlap, with a given model involving a variety of abstract structures.

A stimulus in one of the three categories outlined, impinges upon one or more of the five senses. The amount of attention that it invokes depends upon the stimulus ambiguity which motivates a search for further information. Subject to the perceptual bias brought about the interaction of attitudes and retained motives, the information is received. This informational inputs may alter the existing configuration of motives and choice criteria and thereby modify or disturb the brand attitude, brand comprehension, Purchase intention and/or action. Whether the buying decision is, actually made or not depends upon the interplay of comprehension of the brand attributes, strength of attitudes towards the brand, confidence in the purchase- decision and intention (which in turn are affected by the various exogenous variables like the Importance of purchase influence of culture and family, financial status, etc.).

Q10. It is bent upon buying a pair of jeans. Discuss the factor influencing the decision.

Ans. In social psychology, attitudes are defined as learned, global evaluations of a person, object, place, or issue that influence thought and action.[7] Put more simply, attitudes are basic expressions of approval or disapproval, favourability or unfavourability, or as Bem put it, likes and dislikes.

(1) Decision Sciences: Consumer choice or decision is one- of the most important areas of marketers interests. While economics and psychology (through cognitive psychology) have developed in this area, the emerging discipline of Decision Sciences focusses upon it, most directly. The advantages of this discipline in the area of consumer behaviour are many. (i) This helps in tracking the flow of consumer decision making process; (ii) it helps in sorting out the important attributes or features contributing to the decision; (iii) it helps in understanding tradeoffs among these key attributes and their levels employed in the minds of consumers. Another by product of utilising decision sciences. paradigm in. consumer behaviour is the availability of decision sciences methodologies to consumer behaviour.

(2) Anthropology: Anthropology itself had been preoccupied with, much broader issues like impact of wheel on society or distribution of blood groups across population etc. For the reasons of making its studies more scientific- and isolating the extraneous variables from the main variable of interest, they had often set up their labouuuratories among the isolated tribals located in remote areas. Such things gave to anthropology an esoteric aura. However, there is a growing realisation, both among anthropologists and marketers, to cone closer and gain from the mutual interactions. Anthropologists, on their part, have started studying the phenomena which are commonplace in marketing and no longer overlook them as mundane or difficult to scientifically capture through their established methodologies. Many of these effects may be intended or not. But, they happen nevertheless. Marketers are realising that anthropological understandings of consumers in the context of their products provide them with the cutting edge over their competitors. At another level, the deeply satisfying relationship between the marketing mix, so designed, and their consumers help to retain the customers far longer durations and spread positive word of mouth.

(3) Systems Dynamics and Simulation: System dynamics and simulation have been developed basically to model complex situations. The tools of these techniques are specially honed to handle large number of variable and their relationships. Consumer behaviour situations very closely fit these requirements. As a result, there is a growing appreciations and utilisation of system dynamics and simulation in consumer behaviour models. These disciplines are used for formulating, testing and refining. the models,

Support of Analytic Techniques: Consumer behaviour models -invariably -deal with a multiplicity of variables. For coping with this situation; current consumer behaviour models are using diverse analytical techniques. Most of these techniques were available in the literatures of mathematics, statistics and operations research. But, with the easy availability of sophisticated computing power, these techniques have started playing much greater roles recently. Thus, for example, stepwise regression analysis, correspondence analysis are very often used for identifying the salient variables and their relationships out of the observed data: Factor analysis and multidimensional scaling techniques are used for reducing data and drawing the essence from a large set of data. Very often consumers evaluation of different attributes and their relative trade - offs are important. Conjoint analysis has come as a handy tool for such purposes.

Social cognition is a growing area of social psychology that studies how people perceive, think about, and remember information about others. Person perception is the study of how people form impressions of others. The study of how people form beliefs about each other while interacting is known as interpersonal perception.

QUESTION PAPERS

MS-61 : CONSUMER BEHAVIOUR
June, 2020

Note: (i) Attempt any three questions from Section-A.
(ii) Section-B is compulsory.
(iii) All questions carry equal marks.

Section—A

Q1. (a) Compare and contrast the buying behaviour of final consumers and organizational buyers. In what ways are they most similar and in what ways are they most different?

(b) What do you understand by the term 'Reference Groups'? How do reference groups influence how we behave? Discuss giving suitable examples.

Q2. (a) Why are marketers concerned about customer attitudes? Discuss with the help of suitable examples.

(b) What is meant by Consumer Perception? Explain the stages in the perceptual process.

Q3. (a) Explain the 'Trait Theory of Personality'. What are its limitations?

(b) Define culture and subculture. How is the study of cultural values relevant to a marketer?

Q4. Write short notes on any three of the following:

(a) Applications of consumer behaviour in marketing

(b) Maslow's Hierarchy of Needs

(c) Classical Conditioning

(d) Theories of post-purchase evaluation

(e) Nicosia's model of consumer decision process

Section—B

Q5. (a) In designing the advertising for a soft drink, which would you find more helpful: information about consumer demographics or about consumer lifestyles? Give examples of how you would use each type of information.

(b) Briefly explain the concept of 'Family Life Cycle'. Which stage of the family life cycle could constitute a lucrative segment for the following? Give reasons for your answer:

(i) Home Appliances

(ii) Fashion Clothing

(iii) Luxury Vacation

❑❑❑

MS-061 : CONSUMER BEHAVIOUR
February, 2021

Note: Attempt any three questions from Section A. Section B is compulsory. All questions carry equal marks.

Section—A

Q1. (a) What do you understand by the term 'consumer behaviour'? Discuss the applications of consumer behaviour in designing the marketing mix.

(b) Explain the AIO Inventories method for studying lifestyle, giving suitable examples.

Q2. (a) What is organisational buying behaviour? Explain its characteristics.

(b) You are the marketing manager of a company that sells washing machines. How will you respond to the post-purchase feelings of your customers?

Q3. (a) Explain the term 'information processing' and discuss its marketing implications.

(b) Define culture and subculture. How does subcultural analysis help a marketer in the segmentation exercise?

Q4. Write short notes on any three of the following:

(a) Stages in the perceptual process

(b) Maslow's hierarchy of needs

(c) The functions of consumer attitude

(d) Theories of learning

(e) Trait theory of personality

Section—B

Q5. (a) What is a reference group? Name two reference groups that are important to you. In what ways do they influence you in your purchasing behaviour? Discuss taking example of any product of your choice.

(b) Briefly explain the family life cycle concept. Which stage(s) of the family life cycle would be an attractive segment for the following products and why?

(i) Life insurance policy

(ii) Fast food restaurants

(iii) Luxury products

❑❑❑

MS-61 : CONSUMER BEHAVIOUR
June, 2021

Note: (i) Attempt any three questions from Section-A.
(ii) Section-B is compulsory.
(iii) All questions carry equal marks.

Section—A

Q1. (a) Briefly explain the various elements of external environment that influence consumer behaviour.

(b) Discuss the applications of lifestyle marketing giving suitable examples.

Q2. (a) With the help of examples explain the various organisational buying situations.

(b) Discuss the relevance of studying the sensory system in marketing of goods and services.

Q3. Take the example of purchase of any consumer durable by your family. Explain the decision process with the help of Howard Sheth Model.

Q4. Write short notes on any three of the following:

(a) Theories of post-purchase evaluation
(b) Motivational conflicts
(c) The constituents of consumer attitude
(d) Marketing applications of understanding consumer learning
(e) The theory of self concept

Section—B

Q5. (a) Explain the different roles played by different family members in making buying decision by taking the example of following products:

(i) T. V.
(ii) Cooking Oil

(b) Define culture and sub-culture. Taking any product of your choice explain how subcultural analysis can be used for market segmentation.

❑❑❑

MS-61 : CONSUMER BEHAVIOUR
December, 2021

Note: (i) Attempt any three questions from Section-A.
(ii) Section-B is compulsory.
(iii) All questions carry equal marks.

Section—A

Q1. (a) What is lifestyle marketing? With the help of suitable examples, discuss the applications of lifestyle marketing.

(b) What is organisational buying behaviour? Explain its typical characteristics.

Q2. (a) How is the concept of motivation relevant to our understanding of consumer behaviour? Discuss.

(b) Define personality. What are the differences of 'The Trait Theory' and 'The Psychoanalytic Theory' of personality?

Q3. (a) Discuss the impact of physical surroundings and social surroundings on consumer behaviour in a retail outlet.

(b) Discuss the applications of consumer behaviour in marketing.

Q4. Write short notes on any three of the following:

(a) The functions of consumer attitude

(b) Theories of learning

(c) The family lifecycle concept

(d) The characteristics of culture

(e) Howard Sheth model

Section—B

Q5. (a) How does consumer decision process vary with the nature of the product? Discuss with reference to the purchase of the following products:

(i) Chocolate bar

(ii) Services of a doctor

(iii) Washing machine

Would the process be the same in case of a repeat purchase? Discuss.

(b) What is a reference group? Name two reference groups that are important to you. In what ways do they influence you in your purchase behaviour?

www.ingramcontent.com/pod-product-compliance
Ingram Content Group UK Ltd.
Pitfield, Milton Keynes, MK11 3LW, UK
UKHW021658190726
13853UKWH00001B/339

9 789355 544315